Rod Hogg (signature)

SPEED THRILLS

**RODNEY HOGG
JON ANDERSON**

Cricket's fastest ever bowlers on bouncers, batsmen and serious pace

Dear Patrick:
Rodney Hogg is a lunatic.
Best wishes
Jon Anderson.

PUBLISHED BY AFFIRM PRESS IN 2015

28 Thistlethwaite Street, South Melbourne, VIC 3205.
www.affirmpress.com.au

National Library of Australia Cataloguing-in-Publication entry available
for this title at www.nla.gov.au

Title: Speed Thrills: Cricket's fastest ever bowlers on bouncers, batsmen and
serious pace / Rodney Hogg & Jon Anderson, authors.

ISBN: 9781922213709 (hardback)

Cover and internal design by Karen van Wieringen
Typeset in 10/15 Avenir by D'fine Creative
Printed in China through the Australian Book Connection

SPEED THRILLS

**RODNEY HOGG
JON ANDERSON**

Cricket's fastest ever bowlers on bouncers, batsmen and serious pace

ONLY A FAST BOWLER COULD UNDERSTAND THE
sheer adrenalin rush you get watching a batsman flinch away from
one of your thunderbolts.

If a bowler says that doesn't give them a thrill then they are lying, for
that sight is what bowlers strive for. The wicket can come next ball,
but before you splatter a batsman's stumps you need to establish your
superiority over him. I have no doubt that's what Fred 'the Demon'
Spofforth aimed for back in the 1880s, and Harold Larwood during the
bodyline series of 1932/33.

And while I may be accused of bias, surely there is nothing more exciting
in cricket than the sight of a tearaway quick. A great fast bowler has
always been a stunning sight, from Frank Tyson in the 1950s; Wes Hall
in the 1960s; Dennis Lillee, Jeff Thomson and Michael Holding in the
1970s; Malcolm Marshall in the 1980s; Wasim Akram, Allan Donald and
Shoaib Akhtar in the 1990s; through to modern-day speed merchants
such as Mitchell Johnson, Brett Lee and Shaun Tait.

I caught the bug early, after watching Wes Hall bowl to the Victorians at
the MCG in 1960. From the moment I left that ground I was determined
to do everything in my power to emulate my hero. So I bowled bouncers
at Dad morning and night (and Mum, if possible) in our suburban

backyard in Melbourne. It was only a tennis ball but I still gave them both barrels and dreamed of the day I would do the same for Australia.

My desire grew stronger in 1969 when I saw this locomotive named Dennis Lillee bowling for Western Australia at the MCG. It seemed like he was pushing off the sightscreen, such was the length of his run as he galloped to the wicket, long black hair waving in the wind. The radar-like bouncer of John Snow during the 1970/71 Ashes series in Australia increased my fanaticism, and prompted me to start bowling three to four bouncers in a row in my district-level matches for Northcote. Then my obsession hit its high when I saw Jeff Thomson, arguably the most exciting speedster of all, wreck the English in 1974/75.

My own chance came a few years later in 1978/79, and while I was never a 'Typhoon' Tyson or 'Thommo' Thomson, bowling fast for Australia was my idea of bliss.

This book is dedicated to the men of speed. It's not necessarily a matter of who was the finest fast-bowling practitioner (hence the absence of cricketers such as Sir Richard Hadlee and Glenn McGrath), but of who scared the hell out of batsmen. In these pages are words from some of the greatest living speed demons, and the unfortunate batsmen who faced them. Sadly the likes of Harold Larwood, Malcolm Marshall and Sylvester Clarke (described by many in this book as one of the most dangerous of all) are not around to be a part of it, but they are remembered with awe.

So who was the fastest? Well, obviously there is no way to prove it, but if pushed I would say it's a toss-up between Frank Tyson and Jeff Thomson.

Happy reading,

RODNEY MALCOLM HOGG

41 wickets at 12.85 in the 1978/79 Ashes series
(and don't you forget it).

Editor's Note
JON ANDERSON

THIS BOOK EVOLVED FROM A CONVERSATION THAT turned to a typical cricketing debate: who are the fastest bowlers? It's a question every batsman gets asked, as we all want to get an inkling of what it's like to have to react within half a second of a ball being propelled. It's awe-inspiring to watch from the stands as a Dennis Lillee or a Shoaib Akhtar steams in with thunderous intent on a bowler-friendly WACA wicket, and hard to imagine how the batsman must feel as he steels himself.

So a former fast bowler, Rodney 'Hoggy' Hogg, and I decided to interview both the fastest living pacemen and the batsmen who faced them. Our journey began with England's Frank 'Typhoon' Tyson, who rose to fame in the 1950s, and finished with Australia's current firebrand, Mitchell Johnson. Emphasis was placed on either speed or – as in the case of John 'Snowy' Snow – the ability to consistently bowl short balls at lively pace.

Of those approached, only Dale Steyn and Waqar Younis declined to be interviewed – Steyn due to the request coming during his 2015 World Cup campaign, and Waqar for his own reasons. Balfour Patrick Patterson from Jamaica was another bowler identified as belonging to this select group, but his whereabouts are largely unknown in his home country.

Steyn's name was repeatedly mentioned when discussions turned to 'the best' rather than 'the fastest', a description that could also be applied to the legendary West Indian duo Curtly Ambrose and Courtney Walsh. Sir Richard Hadlee could be placed in the same category, although those who faced him early in his career have suggested that he had plenty of raw pace.

The sublime Malcolm Marshall wasn't included because the emphasis was on living pacemen rather than the finest in history, a description that clearly fits Marshall. Another bowler still spoken of with fear is Sylvester Clarke of the West Indies, who created havoc in England and South Africa during his time in those countries with domestic teams. Sadly Clarke died within a month of Marshall in 1999.

To those who did contribute, a warm thank you. They were all generous with their time and frank with their thoughts. Hopefully they take pride in their contribution to one of cricket's greatest pleasures: the sight of a tearaway fast bowler putting the world's best batsmen under the ultimate pressure.

Contents
SPEED THRILLS

MITCHELL JOHNSON

Born 2 November 1981,
Townsville, Queensland

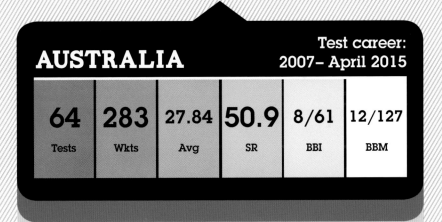

AUSTRALIA

Test career:
2007– April 2015

64	283	27.84	50.9	8/61	12/127
Tests	Wkts	Avg	SR	BBI	BBM

> But what speed guns don't record is the sheer terror of a bowler, and in that regard Johnson belongs right in the upper echelon.

IF YOU WERE TO GO BY THE SPEED GUNS, MITCHELL Johnson would not be listed as the fastest in the game. Quick, yes – in fact decidedly so – yet just that bit short of a Jeff Thomson or Shoaib Akhtar. But what speed guns don't record is the sheer terror of a bowler, and in that regard Johnson belongs right in the upper echelon. When he got it right, as in the Perth Test in 2008 (match figures of 8/61), Johannesburg in 2009 (8/137), Adelaide in 2013 (7/40) and Centurion in 2014 (7/68 and 5/59), few could create more carnage. Batsmen of the calibre of South African duo Graeme Smith and Jacques Kallis, as well as England's Jonathan Trott, were made to move in a manner that was far from composed.

In Smith's case there were a couple of nasty blows to the hand in two Tests in 2009, then a thorough working-over five years later that seemed to hurry his exit from the game. This was after a fine career where he

Johnson's
BEST BOWLERS

WASIM AKRAM

'I'm sure that the same names will keep coming up in the interviews for this book, and Wasim Akram, who I idolised as a kid, would have to be one of them. He would be there for all sorts of reasons: his pace off such a short run, his stamina and obviously his ability to move the ball both through conventional swing and reverse.'

GLENN MCGRATH

'I used to love watching Glenn McGrath bowl. You grow up thinking how great a player is and then you find yourself playing alongside him. It is a big deal and can be a touch overwhelming, but with Glen there was never anything but encouragement. What I learnt from him most was how it helped to remain as calm as you could out on the ground. Now I try to help the younger bowlers too.'

ALLAN DONALD

'Another I rate very highly for his sheer pace and his smooth action.'

ANDY BICHEL AND MICHAEL KASPROWICZ

'With their work ethic, and the way they went about it, they are good examples of how two really good blokes can succeed.'

had taken on, and tamed, the best speedsters on offer. Trott was made to appear just as uncomfortable before he chose to leave the Test scene for a sabbatical during the 2013/14 Ashes series in Australia.

Kallis, ever the master, suffered less, although there was a rearing delivery from Johnson that struck his jaw at Durban on 7 March 2009. It prompted a now famous response from Kallis, a man who usually let his on-field actions speak for him. 'You can prepare for a storm. You can latch all the windows and sandbag the doors. But when the rain comes, it's still a surprise,' he wrote on facing Johnson in 2014. 'At his pace, an uneven surface with up-and-down bounce – and some sideways movement – can be deadly. And yes, I do mean that literally … it was a great challenge. He has always had extreme pace but, in previous tours, he didn't have the accuracy … At the moment he has become the complete bowler with consistent control and exactly the same pace. There's no doubt the South African top order was a bit shell-shocked at Centurion. You can talk yourself to a standstill and watch as many videos as you like in preparation, but there's no substitute for the real thing.'

When Johnson struck Kallis in the same 2009 Test where he broke Smith's hand, setting up a 2/0 lead for Australia in a three-Test series, it signalled his true arrival on the international stage. After his first thirteen Tests, Johnson had averaged a so-so 34.87 with the ball, and while there were some quick moments, the pieces just hadn't quite come together. But it all changed during two Tests against New Zealand in late 2008 followed by six against South Africa. Johnson burst onto centre stage with 47 wickets at 21.17 across these eight matches, plus he scored runs (460 at 46.00), and those runs came quickly. The wickets were just a part of the package given the fear Johnson instilled into opposing batsmen. It made him the most prolific left-handed all-rounder since the incomparable Sir Garfield Sobers.

His approach to the wicket was military in its precision, his arm action slightly slingy, which enabled a bouncer to sometimes explode into very awkward areas. And when he got his inswinger going to right-handers, he became very hard to handle. It appeared Johnson was on his way to a Test career that was going to rival that of Australia's finest all-rounder in Keith Miller. Then, for reasons nobody has ever been able to fully explain, Johnson lost his magic. It was as sudden as Ian Baker-Finch's fall from grace on the golf course, and just as many people weighed in with supposed cures. Johnson spent a couple of years in the wilderness, at times questioning his ability. His woes weren't missed by the English Barmy Army, who developed their own chant whenever Johnson appeared at the bowling crease: 'He bowls to the left/ He bowls to the right/ That Mitchell Johnson/ His bowling is shite.'

> There have been several lethal Johnson spells, with South Africa's Ryan McLaren bearing the full brunt in February 2014.

Sadly for the Barmy Army, and more importantly his opponents, Johnson regained his mojo and again started to put the fear of god into anyone with a bat. Alongside South Africa's Dale Steyn, Johnson finally took his place at the top of the bowling tree, vindicating the faith Dennis Lillee had placed in him years before.

Jacques Kallis of South Africa jumps away from a Mitchell Johnson short ball. Kingsmead, Durban, 2009.

Mitchell Johnson

> 'When I got to age thirteen the normal keeper couldn't keep to me and my mate had to take over.'

After seeing a seventeen-year-old Johnson at a Queensland cricket camp, Lillee had immediately contacted his old teammate Rod Marsh, who arranged a place for Johnson at the Australian Cricket Academy in Adelaide. For Johnson, a kid from Townsville with a hammer in his left hand, it was like a dream.

'I remember playing backyard cricket a lot and I didn't think I was that quick, but I seemed to bowl a lot and never did much batting, so that should have told me something,' recalls Johnson. 'When I got to age thirteen the normal keeper couldn't keep to me and my mate had to take over. So I started to think then that maybe I was getting a bit quicker. I remember playing against Mackay and hitting a kid who wasn't wearing a helmet – and I hit him a couple of times. He was pretty angry and he could also bowl fast, so I was lucky I didn't have to go out and bat.

'Back in my early days I used to love Curtly Ambrose. Everything about him appealed to me: how aggressive he was and how much fun he seemed to be having. Then Brett Lee came along, and all I wanted to do was bowl as fast as "Binga". Then later on to get the chance to play with him was very special for me. I learnt from Binga how important it is to be physically ready so you can keep coming back in the day and bowl with genuine pace in every spell. I have a lot to thank Dennis Lillee for because he has played such a large part in my career and has always been so important.'

Lillee encouraged Johnson to clear his head and just bowl as quickly as he could. He listened well. There have been several lethal Johnson spells, with South Africa's Ryan McLaren bearing the full brunt in February 2014. Playing in just his second Test, and having been bowled

Mitchell Johnson

by Johnson for just eight in the first innings at Centurion, McLaren found himself facing the left-hander in full flight on the fourth day. Twice the South African number seven saw balls scream past his face before a third delivery seemed to explode off a reasonably good length. To McLaren's credit he protected his face only to be struck a very heavy blow on his right ear, sending him to the ground with blood streaming as the medical staff ran to his aid. He batted on but had to be admitted to hospital the next day and played no further part in the series. Six months later he met up with Johnson again, this time in a One Day Tri-series in Harare. The result? A hairline fracture to his forearm. For Johnson it is simply part of cricket, although his instincts were challenged late in 2014 when his teammate and friend in Phillip Hughes was struck and killed in an interstate cricket match at the SCG.

'Phillip's death changed the way I feel. Before Phillip I never wanted to seriously hurt anyone, but I liked to let them know I was after them,' explains Johnson. 'After Phillip I hit Virat Kohli and I didn't feel quite right about it. As time has gone on I'm getting back to my old ways, but it [hitting Kohli] did rattle me and I felt emotional about it. I questioned myself during that period, and it took me some time, most of the summer. I have to play aggressively because that's how I play my best cricket. You bowl a short one at them and you're in their head. I love that part of the game. It's great. And I don't think it's ever going to stop.'

> As Pietersen later admitted, the English dressing-room was filled with fear at the prospect of doing battle with Johnson.

One player Johnson was keen to get to was controversial English master batsman Kevin Pietersen. They faced each other during the Ashes series of 2013/14, and as Pietersen later admitted, the English dressing-room was filled with fear at the prospect of doing battle with Johnson.

'You very seldom hear people in your own team saying that they

Johnson's
BEST BATSMEN

RICKY PONTING

'I got regular tickets to the Ricky Ponting show when we used to bowl to him in the nets. We would be using new balls and bowling two or three feet over the line, as can happen in the nets. You can understand most batsmen not wanting to face bowling under those conditions, but not Ricky. He would be pulling us with ease. It was unbelievable to watch and I used to think the few spectators who sometimes got a chance to see that witnessed something great.'

SACHIN TENDULKAR

'Started his career years before me, and he was someone I grew up admiring. It was a great thrill to be able to bowl to him and see first-hand just how good he was. Like the great players, he seemed to have more time, and was so well organised. He knew his game inside out.'

BRIAN LARA

'I always thought he was an absolute legend with a bat in his hands, and I did get to bowl to him when I was very young.'

AB DE VILLIERS

'Of the current players he challenges you as a bowler in all the forms of the game. He seems to have more strokes than most other players and is very composed at the crease.'

are physically scared, but our tail-end batsmen were scared,' Pietersen wrote. 'I heard [Stuart] Broad, [James] Anderson and [Graeme] Swann say they were scared. When you've got that, you know that a bloke in the other team is doing damage. I was sitting there thinking, *I could die here in the fucking Gabbattoir.* How could Trotty, this calm, collected buddy of mine, play like that? Get hit like that? Get out like that? I was really worried. I'd been spending a huge amount of time on my own in the nets, but suddenly it didn't seem enough. I had been petrified: if Trotty can get played like that, there is no hope for me, because Trotty is normally so calm and cool.'

Johnson describes the 2013/14 Ashes series as 'the most fun I've had in cricket, I just enjoyed every day of that series'. Pietersen later tweeted it was a case of facing someone whose speed coerced you into doing things with your bat that your brain told you not to, like flashing at wide balls outside off-stump: 'There is a HUGE difference when facing someone at 140km/h compared to 150km/h. When you [sic] facing someone as quick as Mitchell, your instinct occasionally makes you do things you shouldn't.'

Mitchell Johnson

> 'When you [sic] facing someone as quick as Mitchell, your instinct occasionally makes you do things you shouldn't.'

Victorian batsman Brad Hodge, who has seen the best of the past two decades come and go, describes Johnson at his finest as a 'pretty ugly, fiery customer'. 'I wouldn't put him in the sheer pace of an Akhtar, Lee or Tait,' says Hodge, 'probably in a category just slightly below them. But when you talk about his short ball and being left-handed, that is pretty scary. Watching him against England in the Ashes series of 2013/14 would have been scary for anyone. At times you didn't feel like you were playing a lot of the balls as they skidded across you towards the slips. But when he started to swing the ball he became that much more dangerous. If you face a ball at 150km/h that doesn't swing it's hard enough, but normally manageable. But when Johnson was swinging the ball he was a nightmare. There was a One Day series in India when he was really swinging it and seemed to get Yuvraj Singh out every time. He was seriously fast, and you could tell the Indians couldn't deal with it.'

Johnson, a prodigious tennis talent as a youngster, enjoys bowling most when the surface promotes an even contest: 'I love wickets that allow even contests, such as the WACA. Okay it is a fast track, which obviously suits us fast bowlers, but batsmen can score very quickly as well. But I wouldn't say my best or most satisfying spell was at the WACA. The spell in Centurion in 2014, to be able to get 12 wickets in the match was a stand-out for me, given where the sides were at. But I also got eight wickets at the WACA against them, which was also a stand-out. And in Phillip Hughes' first Test series, Dale Steyn was causing mayhem, pinging Mike Hussey all over his body. I was able to hit Smith on the hand, Kallis on the chin and bowled Boucher with a fast yorker before lunch. That was a good spell.'

Mitchell Johnson

19

HOGGY'S VIEW

THERE ARE LESS THAN ten fast bowlers with at least 400 Test wickets, and I see no reason why Mitch Johnson won't join that group, given his athleticism and ability to take large clumps of wickets very quickly. When he gets it right he is as good as anyone, it's just that his career hasn't been as consistent as a Richard Hadlee or a Dennis Lillee. Unlike those two he didn't reinvent himself, and at thirty-three he is still pounding in and making divots in the turf. Not many bowlers can get away with not having to compromise their pace but Johnson and Brett Lee are two blokes who just kept sending down the thunderbolts. What you see with Mitch is batsmen playing at balls two feet outside their off-stump, which is a result of his sheer pace drawing them into the shot. They don't have the reaction time to withdraw their bats.

I don't know him well, but like a lot of the bowlers I have interviewed for this book, he seems a charming type of person. In fact I'm the only one who isn't, which worries me. You go in thinking you have to be a mongrel to succeed, and then you meet all these gentlemen – Frank Tyson, Sir Wes Hall, Mike Procter, Michael Holding, Wasim Akram, Shane Bond, Brett Lee – and you wonder why you were snarling all the time.

Mitchell Johnson

But at least on the field most of them are nasty, and Mitch has a bouncer that can be lethal: right up there with the best I've seen, alongside a John Snow or Malcolm Marshall. I have long admired him from afar, except in the 2013/14 Ashes series when he started to get close to my record of 41 wickets against England in Australia. Fortunately he didn't go berserk in Sydney and finished with 37, so I'm safe and I can still go around boring people with my '41 wickets at 12.85, and don't you forget it'.

Not many bowlers can get away with not having to compromise their pace but Johnson and Brett Lee are two blokes who just kept sending down the thunderbolts.

India's Virat Kohli (centre) and Ajinkya Rahane (left) exchange words with Mitchell Johnson. MCG, Melbourne, 2014.

Mitchell Johnson

MICHAEL HOLDING

'Whispering Death'

Born 16 February 1954, Half Way Tree,
Kingston, Jamaica

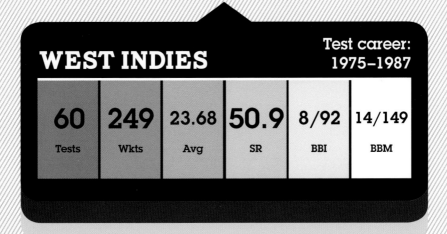

WEST INDIES

Test career:
1975–1987

60	249	23.68	50.9	8/92	14/149
Tests	Wkts	Avg	SR	BBI	BBM

> That apt sobriquet was bestowed upon the Jamaican by English umpire Dickie Bird, because while he couldn't always hear Holding approaching the wicket, he had a bird's-eye view of the carnage the man could cause.

SUCH A MOVEMENT OF BEAUTY WAS MICHAEL Holding's approach to the bowling crease that batsmen were lulled into a false sense of security, doubting that someone so graceful could produce something so menacing.

But as his nickname of 'Whispering Death' implied, Holding was capable of extreme pace. That apt sobriquet was bestowed upon the Jamaican by English umpire Dickie Bird, because while he couldn't always hear Holding approaching the wicket, he had a bird's-eye view of the carnage the man could cause. The cricket ball was released at speeds estimated to regularly be over 150km/h, and on certain days around the magical 160km/h.

He arrived at a time when the finest group of fast-bowling talent was assembled by a single cricketing nation: Holding, Courtney Walsh and Patrick Patterson from Jamaica; Sylvester Clarke, Wayne Daniel,

Michael Holding

Joel Garner and Malcolm Marshall of Barbados; Antiguans Curtly Ambrose and Andy Roberts; Ian Bishop of Trinidad and Tobago; and the venomous Colin Croft of Guyana.

By unanimous verdict Holding was the quickest. His bowling in the first six to seven years of his Test career, which began in 1975, is considered the equivalent of the great speed merchants before him, from Harold Larwood to Frank Tyson, Sir Wes Hall and Jeff Thomson. But with Holding or 'Mikey', as he is known and loved, there was a difference in culture, his bowling more Beethoven than Rolling Stones.

It all began in Kingston, Jamaica, in a game only the locals would understand. Called 'Catchy Shubby', or 'to push out of the way', it just requires a bat, ball, anything for a wicket and open space. 'It was a game where you didn't wear pads and you only got a bat when you bowled whoever was batting,' Holding explains. 'It wasn't any good having them caught, because the catcher would get to bat. If they decided to stand in front of whatever we used for the wicket – sometimes it was a tin pan or corrugated iron – and you hit them on the leg, there was no LBW. So we bowled fast so that when it hit their leg it hurt.

'And bowling fast did seem natural to me. I don't think you can teach someone how to bowl really fast, although you can teach them some of the other aspects. I used to play other sports such as basketball and running, but I was never that good at running [despite cricket commentators for years maintaining the myth that Holding could have run for his country]. Cricket commentator Tony Cozier got me confused with another bowler named Seymour Newman, who became a wonderful 400m–800m runner. The best I got was representing my class. There were so many other good runners, I would never have represented Jamaica at the Olympics.

'When I was seventeen I started to become a fast bowler. I played three years for the senior team at school. The captain didn't always think I could bowl so he gave every other bowler a go first. Then I got on and took a

Michael Holding

Holding's
BEST BATSMEN

SIR VIV RICHARDS

'He had the lot in terms of skill, competitiveness and mental toughness. And he was always a batsman who was aware of the team situation, more about scoring quickly to give us time to bowl the opposition out than breaking records.'

LAWRENCE ROWE

'Had so much time when he batted.'

IAN AND GREG CHAPPELL

'Ian was an attacking player who would give you a chance by taking the game to the opposition and trying to make it easier for his teammates. He always came across as very team-orientated. But Greg was more reliable in his run-making.'

SUNIL GAVASKAR

'In terms of being hard to get out, Sunil Gavaskar would be right up there. He had such wonderful concentration and plenty of time. I think I would have enjoyed bowling to him more in Australia.'

GEOFF BOYCOTT

'Always a prized wicket. People always ask me about the over I bowled to him at Bridgetown, Barbados, in 1981. Yes, plenty happened in it but I bowled faster on other occasions.'

Michael Holding

26

Andy Roberts, Michael Holding and Wayne Daniel celebrate their 55-run win against England. Headingley, Leeds, 1976.

wicket and kept on taking wickets, so they started to bowl me more. By 1975/76 I was twenty-one and ready to play for my country against the Australians. It was a very big trip for a young man but I learnt very fast.

'In that series they played four fast bowlers [Dennis Lillee, Jeff Thomson, Max Walker and Gary Gilmour] and they totally demolished us, but it started to teach us what you could achieve with an all-pace attack. When we were playing India in the Caribbean after that series, Clive Lloyd set them over 400 in Trinidad and they made 4/406 to win. We played two spin bowlers [Raphick Jumadeen and Albert Padmore] yet lost, which just emphasised that fast bowling was the way to go. If you have good fast bowling you win Test matches.

'When you win Test matches it's a great feeling, and being part of the first ever West Indies team to beat Australia 2/0 in Australia in 1979/80 was one of the best feelings in my career. Some great West Indies teams had been to other parts of the world and won but never to Australia, so it was very big for us.'

Michael Holding

One of the key hurdles for Holding in that series was restricting Australia's elegant number four, Greg Chappell. That the right-hander is rated by some as the second-greatest Australian batsman (behind Sir Donald Bradman) is partly due to his performances against the West Indies' incredible fast-bowling line-ups. In seventeen Tests between 1973 and 1982, he scored 1400 runs at 56.00 with five centuries. In four World Series Cricket Supertests in the West Indies in 1978, he accumulated 45, 90, 7, 150, 113, 104 and 85, or 594 runs at 84.85. He faced them all, including Andy Roberts, Michael Holding, Joel Garner, Wayne Daniel, Colin Croft, Sylvester Clarke and Malcolm Marshall.

For Chappell it was a daunting yet rewarding period: 'Anything over 135km/h is quick, and anything in the 140s, which all of those blokes could bowl, is starting to really test you, because you are at the limit of your decision-making. The ball is getting to you in less than half a second and it's taking you just on half a second to make a decision, so it's really stretching the time frame. If you aren't zeroed in on them you are in trouble. When you get to 135km/h that is the changeover point; you start to think, *this bloke is sharp*. And when you get over 140, good luck. You have to be able to refine your method, otherwise …!

'Michael just ran in and bowled as quickly as he could all of the time.'

'I played against Michael Holding a lot and he was certainly, day in, day out, one of the quickest bowlers I faced. Michael just ran in and bowled as quickly as he could all of the time. There were days when you could get in against Michael. He got me out on a number of occasions, but I would say with sheer speed, once you got in against it, it could work in your favour. Then there was the time he played for Tasmania and I batted against him at Launceston on a dodgy wicket in

Michael Holding

Holding's
BEST BOWLERS

DENNIS LILLEE

'Came back so well after such a serious back injury. He was what you would call the all-round fast bowler because he could do it all with the ball.'

ANDY ROBERTS AND MALCOLM MARSHALL

'Both thinking bowlers, always looking for a new way to dismiss a batsman. Maco [Marshall] might have been just ahead of Andy as a bowler, although that would change depending on who you asked.'

JEFF THOMSON

'Thommo was the quickest I ever saw and very, very exciting – and for scaring people he was the tops. For degree of difficulty he was the hardest, and it wasn't very nice batting against him with no helmet. But he wasn't as dynamic as Dennis Lillee.'

IMRAN KHAN

'Had pace and could do things with the ball. You had others who got a lot of wickets, but you wouldn't say that they were fast. Kapil Dev and Richard Hadlee were two.'

SYLVESTER CLARKE

'Could be very difficult for right-handers but he didn't have a very long career.'

Michael Holding

HITTING BATSMEN

'I didn't want to hurt a batsman, but the bouncer was part of my bowling and if I could intimidate them, then fine. But you didn't want to deliberately hit them.

If you are born with the ability to bowl fast, say around 150km/h, then you aren't going to keep bowling half-volleys. What both batsmen and bowlers realise is it's a part of the game that someone can get hurt. When I was still at school, I think around the age of nineteen, I bowled a bouncer and the batsman got hit because he ducked into it. I remember it clearly because the umpire got very angry with me and made me feel as if I had committed a crime. By that stage I had started to bowl too fast for the school batsmen.

I suppose in 1976 it was as close as it came to being full-on after Tony Greig, who became a good friend, made that comment about making us grovel. I don't think it was a good thing for him to say, although I'm sure he didn't mean it the way it came across. What it did ensure was we bowled really fast all summer, particularly to Tony. There was a lot made of it when they brought Brian Close back into the team at age forty-six but I couldn't go easy on him because my responsibility was to my country. There were times in my career when I knew the pitch was dangerous, such as once in Launceston when I hit Derek Randall on a poor pitch and stopped bowling. I'm not a nasty person.'

Michael Holding

the dark. That was about as scary as it gets. The ground had some pine trees along one side, and as the sun went down it was very hard to pick him up – now you see him, now you don't. Some bounced, some didn't, contributing to forty minutes of the toughest batting I experienced.'

Chappell first faced Holding in Australia in a 1975/76 series, which the home side won 5/1. That Australian team included a Test debutant with rare timing by the name of Graham Yallop, a left-hander who had been coached at Carey Baptist Grammar School by another legendary quick in Frank Tyson. After Australia won that series easily, the West Indies returned home to host India in a series they won 2/1, but one in which they lost a Test after playing two spinners.

It was a long time before the West Indies ever selected two genuine spinners again, much to the chagrin of Yallop, who played seven of his first eight Tests against Holding and company, scoring a highly respectable 496 runs at 45.09. He well remembers Holding from those games: 'By two or three yards Michael Holding was the quickest.

English batsman David Steele bends out of the way of a Michael Holding bouncer. Old Trafford, Manchester, 1976.

Michael Holding

'What I didn't do was try to hook Holding. Around the team we realised there was no way we would have the reflexes to hook him.'

He was the most rhythmical of bowlers and his run-up was a delight to watch, just so long as you weren't up the other end. I faced Jeff Thomson in Brisbane a couple of times and he was very quick, but not as accurate as Holding. He would easily have been around 160km/h. He didn't move the ball that much but I don't think it had time to swing. Andy Roberts and Joel Garner were the nastiest, Garner because of his height and Roberts because his eyes penetrated you. I used to tell myself not to look at him,' Yallop says, laughing.

'I can tell you what I didn't do was try to hook Holding. Around the team we realised there was no way we would have the reflexes to hook him. There was no way I could get the bat back and through the shot before the ball was on to me. So you needed to bail out. I can't think of too many players around the world who tried to hook him. Keith Stackpole would have had he played at the same time. Stacky would hook anything if it was short.

'There is a big difference between a 145km/h ball and a 155km/h ball, to the point where the ball becomes blurred. At the latter speed, if you don't have good reflexes and a fair idea of where the ball is going after it leaves the hand, you have no chance. Facing a district bowler at 135km/h is just sheer relief.'

In 1976 Yallop played his first three Tests against the Windies in Australia, then travelled to the Caribbean two years later, where he played the first two Tests before coming up against Colin Croft in a tour game against Guyana: 'I was on 120 or something and played a similar shot to Phillip Hughes. I played the shot too early and *whack*.

Michael Holding

England's Chris Balderstone is bowled by Michael Holding. The Oval, London, 1976.

I say now that I was lucky it only hit me in the jaw and broke it. The ball before was in the same spot I had hit for four, but the next one was a bit quicker. I missed the third Test and came back in a helmet for the fourth Test.

'By then Roberts, Croft and Garner had gone to World Series Cricket, but they had others like Wayne Daniel and Sylvester Clarke who could be seriously nasty on their days. You tend to forget about some of them, and then someone mentions those two. What I can say about those bowlers is I didn't have a problem with any of them. I always found the West Indies very good on the field and there was no obvious sledging. My memories of them are very good, other than the fact I still occasionally wake up in cold sweats screaming, "Don't hook, don't hook!"'

Michael Holding

'I actually told you a lie before, because I did try and hook Holding just once in a Test in Adelaide, given the short boundaries meant it was my only chance of ever hitting him over the fence. He bowled a couple of overs to me and there was nothing short, so I told myself it was going to come sooner or later. It meant I was almost on the back foot when it eventually came. I got through half the shot before hitting a top edge. The ball went over the keeper and took one bounce before crossing what is a really long boundary. After that I said never again.'

QUICKEST SPELL

'Everyone still talks of that over I bowled to Geoff Boycott in 1981 at Bridgetown, Barbados, but that wasn't the fastest I bowled. In 1976 I bowled very quickly but didn't have full control at that stage of my career. There were a couple of times at the WACA in Perth where I bowled quickly on a pitch that every fast bowler loved. I bowled well and quickly in World Series Cricket [35 wickets at 23.09 in nine games] in what was the toughest competition I played in. A key to bowling fast was how your captain handled you, and I was lucky to have Clive Lloyd when I started. He handled us very well, and no bowler ever had a long spell. You could say that's easy enough when you have four pacemen but he still needed to know when each of us needed a rest. It got to the stage when teams didn't want to bat against us.'

Michael Holding

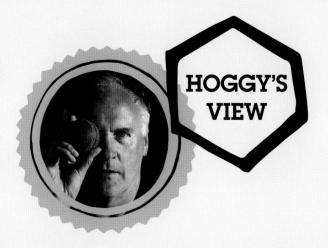

HOGGY'S VIEW

I THINK HE AND THOMMO WERE THE QUICKEST.
Maybe Thommo was a fraction faster because you couldn't pick him
up. In 1961 an artist named Johnny Tillotson recorded 'Poetry in
Motion', and though Mikey was only seven, I swear Tillotson was
singing about his bowling action. I have seen all the greats (some,
like Harold Larwood and Ray Lindwall, on video) and there has never
been a better action. He reminded me of the great 200m–400m runner
Michael Johnson, who seemed to achieve without obvious effort.
Michael Holding glided in and his upper torso was stationary. In some of
the great actions bowling fast involves violent movement, but Michael
never looked in any way violent.

I used to ask him not to bowl too fast to me. At a Test match in the
WACA Michael bowled me a slower ball that I thought was going to be
a quick one. I thought it was a bean-ball. So I turned away a little bit,
then watched as the ball slowly hit the stumps. There may have been
a bit of laughter when I arrived back in the Australian dressing-room.
All I was worried about was ringing my wife to ensure she erased
the video because I didn't want my children to know their father
was a coward.

Michael Holding

35

WASIM AKRAM

'The Sultan of Swing'

Born 3 June 1966, Lahore, Punjab

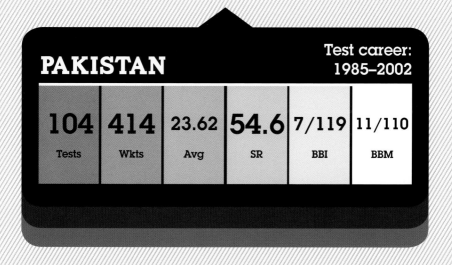

PAKISTAN				Test career: 1985–2002	
104	**414**	23.62	**54.6**	7/119	11/110
Tests	Wkts	Avg	SR	BBI	BBM

Combining an innate ability to swing the ball both ways, a short ball that advised every batsman against rocking on the front foot, and a slower ball that few could pick, Akram is universally regarded as the finest left-arm quick the game has seen.

PICTURE A COUPLE OF HUNDRED TEENAGERS IN THE nets at Lahore, Pakistan, each one waiting for their chance to bowl a ball that may take them onto the international cricketing stage. In 1985 one of those kids was a lad named Wasim Akram, and for six days he dutifully waited for the ball to come his way so he could display his wares.

For six days he went home disappointed, knowing he possessed something that could make them sit up and take notice, but wondering if the chance would arrive. Then, on the seventh and final day, the legendary Pakistani batsman Javed Miandad entered the nets to face the eager youths. Suddenly the ball was thrown to Akram, and after a handful of deliveries a career was born. Miandad saw enough raw potential in the eighteen-year-old to influence the selectors, and Akram was picked for the 1985 tour of New Zealand.

Wasim Akram

Even though Akram now says he didn't know what he was doing, he claimed seven New Zealand wickets in his debut first-class game and 10 wickets in his second Test, signalling the arrival of something special. As green as he was, Akram began with a short sprint to the wicket and extremely quick arm action.

For Australian batsman Dean Jones there was a definite trick to facing Akram, one that involved training your mind to accept that the bloke coming towards you off a very short run-up was actually going to deliver the ball considerably faster than expected.

Combining an innate ability to swing the ball both ways, a short ball that advised every batsman against rocking on the front foot, and a slower ball that few could pick, Akram is universally regarded as the finest left-arm quick the game has seen. There have been others, with Australia's Alan Davidson, the injury-plagued Bruce Reid and more recently the explosive Mitchell Johnson three of the best 'lefties'. Yet Akram's overall record in all forms of the game places him on top. And that may not finish with the left-arm bracket, given enough cricketers of his era unhesitatingly name Wasim Akram when selecting the best fast bowler they have faced.

A fellow card-carrying member of the fast-bowling union in Allan Donald describes the Pakistani as 'the most complete, skilful fast bowler I ever saw and played against'. Indian captain Sourav Ganguly declares, 'Akram is the greatest fast bowler I played against. He is rightly called the "Sultan of Swing".' Even South Africa's Jacques Kallis, statistically the greatest all-rounder the game has seen, agrees: 'In my opinion Wasim Akram of Pakistan was the best pace bowler that I ever faced. Being able to swing the ball both ways with pace made him the most dangerous bowler, and combined with Waqar Younis' reverse-swinging yorkers, bowled with just as much venom, it was a daunting task to play them. Wasim and Waqar in tandem were the best.' New Zealand captain Stephen Fleming also nominates Akram as the best fast bowler.

Akram's nickname 'the Sultan of Swing' is a play on the 1978 hit 'Sultans of Swing' written by Mark Knopfler of Dire Straits. Borrowing heavily from the last verse, in Akram's on-field world it went like this:

And then the man, he steps right up to the bowling crease
And says at last just as the missile leaves on its mission
Gedday, now it's time to go home
And he makes it fast with one more thing,
'I am the Sultan, the Sultan of Swing.'

> 'Facing Wasim Akram was tough. He had the pace and variety, and could out-think batsmen. I was a bunny of Akram early in my career.'

There have been other swing sultans – bowlers such as Ian Botham, Kapil Dev and Terry Alderman – but none could make it bend at the speed Akram could. And every batsman will tell you that when you are facing straight pace, as uncomfortable as it can be, inevitably you get your bearings as long as you can follow the ball in a bowler's run-up. Late swing is always a problem, but if it's arriving around 130km/h then you have a chance. But if it's swinging late and coming at more than 140km/h, good luck.

Two of Sri Lanka's finest users of willow in Kumar Sangakkara and Mahela Jayawardene both rated Akram as top of the pops, Sangakkara saying he had only ever faced a few overs from Akram, and even from that short time saw enough to suggest he was the best. For Jayawardene, 'Facing Wasim Akram was tough. He had the pace and variety, and could out-think batsmen. I was a bunny of Akram early in my career. It was equally challenging against Glenn McGrath and Shane Warne.' Curtly Ambrose, the last of the feared West Indies quicks, who played from 1975–95, also regards Akram as the best for what he could do with the ball at high speed.

Wasim Akram

40

Wasim Akram

Akram's
BEST BATSMEN

SUNIL GAVASKAR

'I only got Sunil Gavaskar out once and he was a prize wicket for me in 1987 because he was the number one batsman in the world at the time and his technique was so solid.'

MARTIN CROWE

'Martin Crowe straight away comes to mind. Waqar and I both agree he was outstanding at handling the reverse swing. He got two hundreds in 1993 and really stood out with his class. Such a straight technique.'

MARK TAYLOR

'Of the Australians who handled me best with the new ball it would have to be Mark Taylor. He used to leave the ball so well which was very frustrating.'

ANDY FLOWER

'Another with a very good technique against reverse swing plus he had a big heart. I hit him quite a few times but he kept getting on the front foot.'

What of Brian Lara, a left-hander like Akram, and also like Akram a claimant to the title of best in his area of expertise (in Lara's case, batting in a highly entertaining fashion and often for long periods)? 'Over my fifteen or sixteen years of playing international cricket in Tests and One Day Internationals, Wasim Akram is definitely the most outstanding bowler I ever faced.'

Then there is 'the Little Master', India's incomparable Sachin Tendulkar, who ended his career with fifty-one Test centuries from two-hundred matches. Tendulkar first saw Akram in 1989 while making his debut as a sixteen-year-old in Pakistan and facing the Akram and Younis team at its fiery best. Tendulkar got on strike to Akram for the third ball of the over, which was an extremely brutal bouncer. Even at that age Tendulkar was a student of his opponents and thought he knew the next one would be a screaming yorker. Wrong. Another bouncer, and for good measure so were the last two balls of the over. Tendulkar momentarily wondered if he had what it took to succeed at Test level, fears that would be put to rest in time.

For Akram it was just a matter of achieving what he had always wanted, but not something he could have done without the guidance of Imran Khan. 'I always wanted to be a fast bowler, even when I was a boy bowling the streets of Lahore. It was my dream to be like Imran Khan on and off the field. He was my idol, and the first time I was next to him in the dressing-room I couldn't even speak because I was so nervous, so in awe of him. But he spoke to me straight away about what I should do, saying, "Run in quick and bowl as quickly as you can, because if you have pace, there is no point in bowling line and length,"' Akram explains.

'He taught me how to use the crease, how to get my run-up right, how to bowl with the new ball, how to bowl with the old ball, adjusting to different pitches. So he helped me enormously. But playing for Lancashire was also of great benefit because I was playing cricket twelve months of the year.

Wasim Akram

Alec Stewart of England avoids a bouncer from Wasim Akram. The Oval, London, 1996.

'It was Javed Miandad who picked me up out of the blue while I was a net bowler. He liked what I was doing and got me on the tour to New Zealand where I got some wickets in my second Test. That tour of New Zealand was my debut in first-class cricket. I got 7/15 and picked up John Wright, Jeff Crowe, Martin Crowe, Jeremy Coney and Geoff Howarth, I still don't know how. A few weeks later I was bowling against the Australians at the MCG, which is a ground that has been kind to me in both Test and One Day cricket. Back then I didn't know what I was doing, just running in and bowling as fast as I could and hoping. For an eighteen-year-old from Lahore it was unbelievable playing at the G.

'Imran gave me a secret, explaining that if a match is about to draw and your body is really tired, run in and bowl three or four more overs because it will make your muscles stronger and you will start to bowl quickly, which I did. Almost every delivery, Imran would speak to me from mid-off – a dream come true. I remember this magazine called *Cricket Digest Monthly*, there were these names of players who bowled fast like Dennis Lillee, Jeff Thomson, Malcolm Marshall and Rodney Hogg. So for me I realised in 1988 that I had pace and I could scare batsmen, and I enjoyed that feeling. I was there to intimidate the batsmen, hit them if I could, upset them.'

Wasim Akram

One of those batsmen struck by Akram was the world's finest leg spinner, Shane Warne. The respect between the pair is mutual, Warne describing Akram as the best he faced. 'To me, Wasim was probably the best fast bowler I played against, the cleverest and most skilful. Glenn McGrath was the best I played with, although I'm very biased towards him. Wasim was such a clever bowler, and he's a clever person. Curtly Ambrose was all quality, but as far as all skills go, reverse swing, around the wicket, over the wicket and also if he wanted to stick one up you or hit you on the head, Wasim could,' Warne says, laughing.

> 'I don't know what the speed gun said, but when he was "on" he was around 145km/h plus.'

'He probably bowled the fastest spell I faced in twenty-three years of cricket at that level. It was in October 1994 at Rawalpindi, in a Test match. It was unbelievable. I don't know what the speed gun said, but when he was "on" he was around 145km/h with such a fast arm. He could really crank it up when he wanted to, 145km/h plus. And once you are over 140km/h it is quick. It was bowlers like Wasim and Waqar that prompted me to hold my bat high in the backlift. Those two broke my toes with those fast in-swinging yorkers, so I had to change something and it did help. I didn't get hit on the head much, but he got me twice. I remember batting with Paul [Pistol] Reiffel at the SCG when Wasim hit me in the head trying to take an easy single, and Pistol just said, "NO," as he rested on his bat. There was no way I could talk him into it.'

Dean Jones has no doubt Akram is the best exponent of his craft the game has seen: 'He was quick enough, don't worry about that, and when you move it both ways at pace then it becomes a problem. He had more movement than anybody who bowled at his pace. Plus he could swing it conventionally and reverse it. Who were

Akram's
BEST BOWLERS

MALCOLM MARSHALL

'The most complete bowler of all time. He was the only bowler who toured Pakistan and consistently got wickets and that is how I rate a bowler, players who got wickets on different surfaces all around the world. Some lose heart when they bowl on some surfaces and become ineffective.'

SHOAIB AKHTAR

'Very sharp, and I saw him close-up because I captained him for five years. He was a bit of a rebel off the field. All he wanted to do was bowl quick. What Imran did for me, I did for Shoaib.'

WAQAR YOUNIS

'A very effective partner. When we bowled we didn't worry about the speed gun like they do today. As soon as they bowl they want to look up to see their speed. We never bothered about that because all we wanted to do was take wickets rather than bowling 150km/h plus. And if you want to swing the ball, you have to reduce your speed. And that's how you can deceive batsmen. The key to developing as a quick bowler is to first learn how to swing and then build up speed, not the other way round. If you can swing at a high speed, you will be unplayable.'

the great swing bowlers? 'Beefy' [Ian] Botham could swing it, so could Damien Fleming. Then there was Darren Gough and of course Terry 'Clem' Alderman, but they weren't anywhere near as quick as Wasim. He is the greatest left-arm bowler ever, simple, with Alan Davidson the only person who got near him. And he could bowl a really good short ball with no obvious backlift in his arm.

> 'He is the greatest left-arm bowler ever, simple, with Alan Davidson the only person who got near him.'

'The difference with the Pakistani bowlers in Wasim and Waqar and the West Indians is against the latter you had to be very good in the top half of your body because they were trying to knock your block off, whereas with the Pakistanis you had to be supple in the bottom half because they were trying to knock your toes off. Three things in sport I've learnt, when the Chicago Bulls were in trouble, they threw the ball to Michael [Jordan], when Manchester United was in trouble, they got the ball to George [Best], and when Pakistan was in trouble, they brought Wasim back on.

'His batting shouldn't be forgotten either. I can remember taking him to a cricket camp where a bunch of kids were invited to ask questions. The first question was, "What was your top score in Tests, Wasim?" to which he proudly replied, "257 not out." Then this other kid, his name might have been Johnny, piped up with, "Who was it against Wasim?" to which he had to admit it was Zimbabwe, prompting the boys to say it didn't count.'

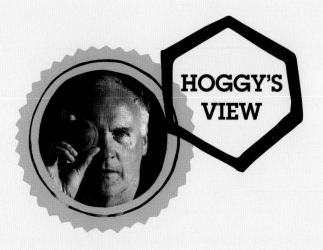

HOGGY'S VIEW

ONE OF HIS FIRST GAMES WAS THE ONE DAY
International under lights at the MCG in February 1985. We should have known he was something special as he had already taken 10 wickets in just his second Test at Carisbrook, Dunedin, in New Zealand. He was an eighteen-year-old kid who created a huge impression right from the start. He bowled three of our batsmen in Robbie Kerr, Kepler Wessels and Dean Jones, got Kim Hughes caught, plus he had Allan Border hit wicket, which normally tells you the bowler is a bit quicker than the average. He ended up with 5/21 on his way to becoming the best bowling all-rounder the game has seen. If you doubt that then argue against him being the best left-arm bowler ever.

What I always wondered was how he generated such pace from such a short run-up. He had a very fast arm action and very economical style. Didn't Shane Warne say he was the fastest he

> We should have known he was something special as he had already taken 10 wickets in just his second Test at Carisbrook, Dunedin, in New Zealand.

Wasim Akram

ever faced? And Warnie batted against Allan Donald, Shoaib Aktar and Waqar Younis. I think with Wasim there was deception and he caught many batsmen out by the pace he got onto them. They say you can't get any quicker off the pitch but I reckon Wasim is one who might have. He really skidded off and got so many LBWs and batsmen bowled. They seemed to get constantly caught at the crease. And if people don't think he was quick enough to be in this book then they never faced him. I always rated how quick they were by how scared I used to get as they ran in. Jeff Thomson I was 10/10, like totally petrified. Michael Holding 9/10, and with Wasim I was around 7.5/10, and he was only eighteen. I'm sure it would have pushed out to 9/10 as he got older. It's funny with left-arm bowlers because very few of them have been super quick. Probably just Wasim and Mitchell Johnson.

Wasim Akram celebrates Pakistan's World Cup Final victory against England. MCG, Melbourne 1992.

Wasim Akram

ALLAN DONALD

'White Lightning'

Born 20 October 1966,
Bloemfontein, Orange Free State

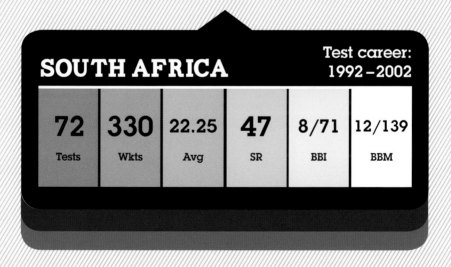

SOUTH AFRICA				Test career: 1992–2002	
72	330	22.25	47	8/71	12/139
Tests	Wkts	Avg	SR	BBI	BBM

To whisper a name is a sign of great cricketing respect, the equivalent of the Mafia lowering their voices when discussing a rival hit man.

ALLAN DONALD WAS BORN TO BOWL FAST: A YOUNG man with a right arm that could propel javelins far distances, and who inherited the best athletic traits of his parents, Stuart and Francina. But it took a meeting with a crusty Australian fast bowler to develop the hard edge that would take Donald to the top in international cricket. The day he met Rodney Malcolm Hogg is one Donald will never forget, a memory he kept to the forefront during a career that had his name whispered in dressing-rooms across the world.

For that is what cricketers do when discussing the genuine speed merchants, from Frank 'Typhoon' Tyson to Michael 'Whispering Death' Holding and Allan 'White Lightning' Donald. To whisper a name is a sign of great cricketing respect, the equivalent of the Mafia lowering their voices when discussing a rival hit man. And with ball in hand Donald did become a hit man, although he remained a delightful person off the field. The on-field persona he puts down to a meeting with the Australian team that staged a rebel tour of South Africa in 1985/86 and 1986/87.

Donald's career had been fast-tracked to the point where he made his Orange Free State debut on his last day of school in November 1985. He finished a science exam at 7am before hurrying off to the Ramblers' ground in Bloemfontein. There he opened the bowling against the visiting Australian rebel team under the captaincy of Kim Hughes. Donald far from disgraced himself, claiming the wickets of opening batsman Steve Smith and all-rounder Trevor Hohns, and four days later he was picked to play for the President's XI in Pretoria against the same opposition. And that is where he met Rodney Hogg.

HITTING BATSMEN

'You just feel so much for Phillip Hughes' family and friends, although I'm sure Phillip wouldn't want to change the way a fast bowler targets batsmen. It's part of the game, and that's just the way cricket is. Being able to bowl a bouncer is a very important part of a player's armoury. Having said that you never want to hurt a batsman. I can remember a country game for Warwickshire when the Glamorgan captain Hugh Morris ducked into a short ball (he was on 233 at the time). For one horrible moment I honestly thought I had killed him, and he was carried off on a stretcher, but fortunately he suffered no lasting damage.'

Morris holds no grudge against Donald: 'I ducked and turned my head and it hit me half on the bottom of the helmet and half on the bottom of the skull and I was knocked out. I got hit on my head quite a few times during my career; in that era it was an occupational hazard for an opening batsman against the battery of the West Indian fast bowlers. But that was my scariest moment and worst incident. I reflected on that after hearing the dreadful news about Phillip. I thought, *there but for the grace of god*.'

Allan Donald

'I look back now and laugh at the memory, even if it didn't seem very funny to an eighteen-year-old at the time,' says Donald. 'I was wearing these ridiculous shorts and walked onto the ground just ahead of Hogg and a couple of his teammates, Steve Rixon and John Dyson. I think there was something said then, but it was in the second innings that Hoggy really got into me. I played and missed quite a few times, and in the end he shouted at me, "Listen, you little —, I'll bounce you back to fucking school." You have to remember I was very inexperienced, and I had never heard anything like that on a cricket field. But it definitely helped toughen me up. A year later I played against the Australians in this goldmining town called Virginia, and when Hogg came out to bat I gave him everything. In fairness he didn't get out and helped win the game for Australia, then afterwards shook my hand and said, "Well bowled." That's the way it should be in cricket, as long as it isn't racial or physical.

'In that game I had been instructed by Roy Pienaar to be really aggressive. He just wanted me to express myself, and I had some confidence because I had just taken eight wickets against the great Clive Rice and company at Transvaal. But it wasn't that easy when you were suddenly playing against these blokes you had been reading about as a kid. Players like Hoggy, Carl Rackemann, Terry Alderman and Rod McCurdy, who was a real nut. I knew I had to compete, to leave a mark on the game that would help me play for South Africa regularly. I knocked Kim Hughes over twice when I bowled him in Port Elizabeth. I was then picked to play alongside Graeme Pollock and Clive Rice, to be in the same dressing-room as the legendary Pollock for his last Test. I got Kim with a little off-cutter that knocked his bail off. It helped my confidence so much.'

> 'I knew I had to compete, to leave a mark on the game that would help me play for South Africa regularly.'

Allan Donald

54

Allan Donald bowls England's Darren Gough a bouncer. England, 1994.

Allan Donald

And it helped launch the career of one of many fine South African fast bowlers, from Peter Heine and Neil Adcock in the 1950s, Peter Pollock and Mike Procter in the 1960s, Vintcent van der Bijl and Garth le Roux in the 1970s and 1980s, and more recently Shaun Pollock, Makhaya Ntini, Dale Steyn and Morné Morkel.

> 'When I first played against Allan Donald I had experienced pace at the different levels as I progressed, but he was just that bit quicker again.'

And to think Donald, who clearly has a fast bowler's physique, once considered bowling leg breaks. It lasted just a few games before a teacher with a few smarts told Donald he required a young tearaway. Many wish that teacher had never opened his mouth, such was the carnage Donald caused during his cricketing journey. Like so many of his kind he was regarded warmly away from a cricket field, and with nervousness on it. Donald crossed the white line and became a win-at-all-costs cricketer, as Australian top-order batsman Matthew Elliott vividly recalls: 'When I first played against Allan Donald I had experienced pace at the different levels as I progressed, but he was just that bit quicker again.

'I was a country boy from Lancaster near Kyabram in Victoria's north, and it wasn't until I came down to Melbourne for district cricket that I realised the difference. I was playing for Collingwood against Waverley/Dandenong in my first game, and they had this old bloke called Rodney Hogg who hit the bat really hard. But he was still complaining because he reckoned the wicket wouldn't allow him to bowl his throat ball. Five or six years later I'm facing Donald in Johannesburg in a Test match. That particular Test was one of my fleeting moments in the sun when I hit him for six over square leg at the Wanderers. It was a pretty flat wicket, thank god, and we had a

Donald's
BEST BOWLERS

WASIM AKRAM

'Had it all as a bowler. It didn't really matter what the wicket was doing because he could swing the new ball and reverse it when it got old. And he was quick. When you can swing it at speed it becomes close to impossible for the batsman.'

SIR RICHARD HADLEE

'When I first went to England I got bowled twice by Richard Hadlee, by balls that were close to unplayable. I ended up buying a Richard Hadlee video to find out just how he did it. I didn't realise what was required from a mental point of view, and Hadlee explained how you needed different tactics for each batsman. That video helped me become a far more complete bowler.'

MALCOLM MARSHALL

'Another I watched closely at the beginning of my English career. While he and Hadlee were coming to the end, they both used the crease so well and swung it late. Plus his control of the slower ball was outstanding.'

DALE STEYN

'The bee's knees: so focused, so professional and always gives it everything. Just look at his strike rate and you realise he sits among the greatest ever. That is truly where he belongs.'

Allan Donald

Donald's
BEST BATSMEN

SACHIN TENDULKAR

'The best. Ahead of the greats of my era like Ricky Ponting and Brian Lara. He always struck me as the most complete batsman, plus he had the best concentration. Importantly he was able to make runs all around the world, proving he could adapt to all conditions.'

MIKE ATHERTON

'This will surprise a few people. I really admired Atherton for his resilience. He didn't have the sheer talent of Lara or Ponting but he was so tough mentally, and that was what I struggled with more.'

STEVE WAUGH

'Waugh would be ahead of Atherton, but only when it came to fighting for their wicket. They both played deep in their crease, and it was vital to make them play. They didn't really want you bowling at them.'

MARTIN CROWE

'Someone who played very straight and knew when to leave the ball. Plus he had the patience that the greats need.'

Allan Donald

pretty good tussle that day. I got 80 odd [85 from 113 balls when batting at three] and then the next game was on a green top at Port Elizabeth.

'Donald is rightly remembered for his exceptional pace, but he was also a great athlete with serious stamina. He seemed very flexible and ran beautifully. You always knew you were in the contest and there weren't too many smiles, but he was never over the top in his sledging. I batted for about an hour and kept thinking, *he can't have another one*, but he kept walking up from fine leg taking his hat off. It's one thing to be quick but to be able to keep reproducing it over an extended spell – a session, a day, four days – that sets the great ones apart. In that series he got me three times in three Tests.

'I didn't always choose to hook someone that fast early in the day. I wore a helmet with the ear piece and without the full grill, which meant I didn't rely on the helmet to do the work. You have to be that little bit sharper again and you have to watch the ball that little bit closer. Devon Malcom on a given day was in the same pace bracket as Donald. Shaun Tait was another who could bowl a very good spell, and I remember Matthew Nicholson bowling really fast to me at the WACA. Courtney Walsh and Curtly Ambrose were quick and great bowlers, but not as quick as Donald, although when I faced them they were towards the end of their careers. You can tell from the first ball when someone is that little bit quicker – Darren Gough could bowl some quick spells – but really it can come down to when and where you catch them. Shoaib Akhtar was the quickest I faced and hit the bat very hard. He would push you back in the crease before you looked to come forward. You try to make the pitch as long as possible when you are facing bowlers like Donald and Akhtar.'

Elliott's Victorian teammate Brad Hodge may only have six Tests to his name, but as the shorter forms of the game have become more popular, his unique batting skill set has taken him around the world. He was playing first-class cricket for his state at age eighteen, a batting

Allan Donald

prodigy identified in the way freakish talents always seem to stand above their peers. It might be their timing, or in Hodge's case an ability to never look rushed against even the quickest bowling. In just his second game for Victoria he came up against Donald and, as kids will do, allowed his natural instincts to take over.

'It probably wasn't surprising given how little senior cricket I had played, but I had never seen that pace before,' says Hodge. 'My first ball I hooked him for six, and the next ball I hooked for four. He then made it particularly clear, in Afrikaans, that it wasn't going to happen again, and for the next few balls he became White Lightning. I had never seen pace like it before. I was this young pup who stirred him up and he fired up very quickly. It probably wasn't a good idea to succeed off the first two, but when you are young it's very much "see it and hit it".

> 'My first ball I hooked him for six, and the next ball I hooked for four. He then made it particularly clear, in Afrikaans, that it wasn't going to happen again.'

'Where does Donald sit in terms of the fastest I have faced? Well, he's up there, no doubt. I faced Devon Malcolm in Bendigo with bad sightscreens and a storm coming. We should have gone off but because there were a few people there the umpires decided we had to stay out. I remember I edged one and it went straight to Michael Atherton at second slip, who was miles back. He didn't see it and it hit him straight on the chest, and it bounced straight up there. Graham Thorpe caught it and I was pretty much happy to go.'

Of course it could have all been very different for Donald had he followed the lead of Robin Smith and Allan Lamb by leaving South Africa to become an English citizen. Donald was well aware apartheid had reduced Mike Procter to seven Tests and Barry Richards to four, and there were no guarantees the Test ban was going to be lifted in Donald's playing career. 'I got a contract in 1987 to play for Warwickshire and it was around that time that Allan Lamb and Robin Smith asked me if I wanted to play for England. We didn't know what was going to happen with South Africa and I almost ended up playing for England. But there were some key people in South Africa who advised me to wait, and fortunately I did,' recalls Donald.

By remaining a South African player, Donald had the chance to play alongside recalcitrant West Indian quick Sylvester Clarke for Free State in the Currie Cup. Clarke was a large, brooding man who didn't always seem to like people, or at least those who happened to be holding a bat and facing him. He played just eleven Tests for the West Indies in an era where they seemed to grow quicks on trees, but it seemed wherever he plied his trade, whether in his native Barbados, English County side Surrey or in the Currie Cup in South Africa, mayhem ensued. His bowling could be vicious, as 942 first-class wickets at 19.52

Michael Atherton of England avoids a bouncer from Allan Donald. The Oval, London, 1994.

Allan Donald

> '**Donald is rightly remembered for his exceptional pace, but he was also a great athlete with serious stamina.**'

would suggest. Donald remains in awe of the man he calls 'Sylvers' to this day.

'He was a great guy once you got to know him but he was frightening, the most frightening I have seen. He used to bowl these huge inswingers and then a short one that kept following the batsman. And he would bowl wide of the crease and once he got his range he could be devastating. He hit a lot of batsmen over a long period of time, probably as many as anyone, and I don't think it worried him too much,' says Donald. Sadly Clarke died of a heart attack aged forty-four in 1999, just three weeks after Malcolm Marshall was taken by cancer.

'I think playing with Sylvers honed my aggression, although I was naturally like that on the field. I wanted to be as hard and ugly as possible because I quickly learnt that the guys I played with and against, like Clive Rice, were mean on the cricket field. At Test level most don't survive unless they have that edge.'

Allan Donald

HOGGY'S VIEW

ALLAN SHOULD BE THANKING ME FOR GIVING HIM those fashion tips back in 1985, because the shorts he was wearing were embarrassing. As is often the case, I was putting others ahead of myself and only thinking of him, although I may also have let him know what was about to happen when he faced me. But once again, I was only thinking of his career and how I could help fast-track it.

Actually, I had forgotten that we first played in 1985 and that I had sledged him so much. It now makes sense, because the next year at that goldmining town called Virginia he gave me two beamers. I remember thinking, *who is this lunatic*? And they were quick. Then he bowled Kim Hughes in that unofficial 'Test' in Port Elizabeth, and if you look through Kim's dismissals in Test cricket you will find he was rarely bowled. Caught, yes, but hardly ever bowled because his defence was so good. Allan had these boots that didn't look remotely like cricket boots should, but he could still bowl really fast. I wish there was a photo of him now with those shorts and boots.

My other vivid memory of Allan is watching him bowl really fast leg cutters at Edgbaston against Australia. Very few could bowl really fast leg cutters. Dennis Lillee springs to mind, but even Dennis didn't bowl them at the pace of Allan Donald.

Allan Donald

63

DENNIS LILLEE

Born 18 July 1949, Subiaco,
Perth, Western Australia

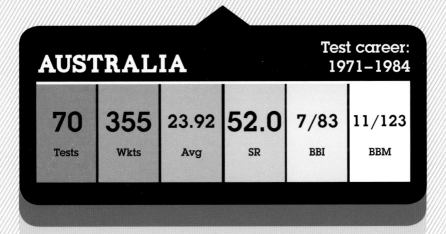

AUSTRALIA

Test career:
1971–1984

70	355	23.92	52.0	7/83	11/123
Tests	Wkts	Avg	SR	BBI	BBM

Lillee is viewed as the ultimate competitor, a player who always demanded his captain throw him the ball, even when his body, or more precisely back, told him to stop.

HE IS BEST REMEMBERED AS AN ABSOLUTE MASTER OF his craft, someone who took an honours degree in fast bowling that in another profession could have led to the lofty tag of 'Professor Dennis Lillee', such is the esteem in which he is held.

Lillee is viewed as the ultimate competitor, a player who always demanded his captain throw him the ball, even when his body, or more precisely back, told him to stop. That desire, coupled with an ability to continually adapt to a variety of conditions, is the main reason that Lillee's name is always to the fore whenever cricket historians sit to ponder their dream attack. He's up there with the likes of Wasim Akram, Sir Richard Hadlee, Sydney Barnes and Malcolm Marshall.

Unlike some others in this book, who almost fell into fast bowling after beginning their careers as batsmen and wicketkeepers, Lillee was fast from day one. As his Australian and Western Australian teammate

Keith Stackpole
ON LILLEE

'Early on he was really quick, not as quick as Thommo (Jeff Thomson) or Gordon Rorke, but he was very sharp. All over the place, though, even when he took those five wickets in his first Test at Adelaide. He became a much more refined bowler. From what I can gather from my father [Keith Stackpole Senior, a fine Victorian state player] Ray Lindwall early on was a bit like that, but when he came back from England he learnt to do more with the ball: outswingers, inswingers. Change of pace, slow it down a little bit and get more control of the ball. Lindwall and Lillee had beautiful actions.

Dennis probably had two actions, the loose-limbed colt when he began and then very much more controlled after Austin Robertson got hold of him and taught him how to run. He became Carl Lewis with a ball. Who would you take out of Warne or Lillee? I'd take Lillee because he got more top batsmen out. I really believe the MCG taught Dennis how to complete his master's degree in bowling. The ball would only get a foot high so he learnt to do things with it: running his fingers across the seam both ways, slowing it up, shortening his run-up. Take the Tests he missed for Australia [forty through injury and World Series] he would have been up around 550 given he averaged over five wickets per Test, which was unheard of when he played, although it would have been indicative of his standing as a bowler.'

Dennis Lillee

Bruce 'Stumpy' Laird recalls: 'I was a sixteen-year-old batting at number eight for South Perth against this seventeen-year-old named Dennis Lillee, who was bowling very fast for Perth. Dennis ran in and hit my batting partner flush on the emblem of his cap – that's in the days when there were no helmets. The ball reached the boundary on the second bounce, prompting a phone call to a state selector that basically went along the lines of: "You had better get down here quickly because something pretty special is taking place."'

Laird knew then that Lillee was going to play for Australia for a long time, and that his career would begin sooner rather than later: 'He was the best I saw, not just for his natural ability, but for his competitive nature and stamina. The four West Indies quicks used to bowl around eighty overs a day, so Clive Lloyd would be able to keep them fresh and use them in five-over brackets. But Dennis just kept going no matter who was bowling with him.'

Lillee boasted a leg cutter that had no peer (except perhaps Malcolm Marshall's), a change of pace that only the greats seem to truly master and a willingness to experiment, even if it meant giving up a few runs. He would bowl to a plan and more often than not achieve his aim, as can be seen in his volume of work right up to his final Test in 1984, where he claimed eight Pakistani victims at the SCG.

But that was long after the first coming of Lillee, the tearaway quick who burst on the scene against England in 1970/71. On 6 December 1970, with arms flailing, the 21-year-old had showcased his pace in a tour game at the WACA, knocking the cap off revered English opener Geoffrey Boycott. On the back of that spell, Lillee made his Test debut at the Adelaide Oval for the sixth Test of the series against England. 29 January, to be exact. English captain Ray Illingworth won the toss and batted on a typically even Adelaide pitch. But Lillee, working in tandem with another debutant in big left-arm Queenslander Tony Dell, disappointed nobody with 5/84. Years later Boycott, who was run out for 58, would name Lillee in his greatest team in history.

Dennis Lillee

> Although the first Test ended in a relatively tame draw at the Gabba, 22-year-old Rest of the World opening batsman Sunil Gavaskar saw enough of Lillee to predict the coming decade of terror.

Boycott saw both versions of Lillee: the raw-boned, long-haired kid who just wanted to bowl fast, and the cagey old professional who could make the ball talk and still produce a seriously quick one every so often, particularly when batsmen started to get on the front foot. In the early days, the Perth bank teller was also raw *off* the field, as the Australians quickly discovered on a Second XI tour of New Zealand in 1970. For a couple of weeks, fellow tourists Greg Chappell and Graeme Watson had plenty of harmless fun at the expense of naive Lillee. But once he realised he was being set up, he never forgot, just like with his bowling. A wide-eyed kid returned from New Zealand with a harder edge, even if his bowling would take a little longer to fine-tune.

The original bowling model, with legs and arms flapping as he pounded the turf, was at its most potent in December 1971, when Sir Garry Sobers captained a Rest of the World team that replaced the touring South Africans, who at the time were banned from world cricket for the implementation of the appalling apartheid system.

Although the first Test ended in a relatively tame draw at the Gabba, 22-year-old Rest of the World opening batsman Sunil Gavaskar saw enough of Lillee to predict the coming decade of terror. He also saw sufficient raw speed to prompt him to leave his skilful hook shot in the dressing-rooms. 'Sunny', as he would become known on his way to being the first man to score 10,000 Test runs, shaped to hook a Lillee short ball in the second innings before realising the red missile had thundered into the gloves of keeper Rod Marsh. Even at the end of his career, and after battles against any number of tall West Indians with pace to burn, Gavaskar regarded that ball as right up there with the fastest he ever faced.

Sobers, Gavaskar and team (players of the calibre of Zaheer Abbas, Rohan Kanhai, Clive Lloyd, Tony Greig, Intikhab Alam and Bishan Bedi) travelled to the WACA. There they swiftly concluded that Lillee, who had bowled quickly and taken three wickets in Queensland, was going to be a whole different proposition on one of the fastest wickets in world cricket.

> 'Against the Rest of the World in Perth was probably his fastest spell.'

Doug Walters, who blasted 125 in Australia's first innings total of 349, slept well after that score was posted by stumps on the first day, for he knew things were going to heat up considerably: 'Back then, and particularly in that game, Dennis was a young tearaway up-and-coming quick with enormous potential. I didn't say, like they do today, that this bloke is going to take 250 Test wickets, but I always thought there was something special about him – plus he swung the ball at pace. And he was a great natural competitor. Against the Rest of the World in Perth was probably his fastest spell. That was sheer speed, up there with all of the great West Indians in Michael Holding, Andy Roberts, Malcolm Marshall and Joel Garner.

'In fact the only bloke of that period I could say was definitely quicker than Dennis Lillee was "Thommo" [Jeff Thomson]. It's funny when you hear them all saying how Dennis and Richard Hadlee became better bowlers when they cut their pace. I know when I would rather face them: give me the medium pace versions any day. Not that you ever particularly wanted to face them. Ask the blokes who batted in that

Dennis Lillee

Rest of the World game: Garry Sobers, Clive Lloyd, Sunny Gavaskar and them. I bet they will tell you they wished Dennis was bowling off his shorter run that day.'

For the record, and they are figures that remain at the forefront of any half-decent statistician's mind, Lillee took 8/29 from 7.1 overs that day in Perth, with six of them coming via catches behind the wicket. It rocketed him up the world cricketing grapevine, and while the word didn't travel as fast in those days, there were plenty of international players there to ensure it reached places such as England and the West Indies quickly enough.

It was a fast-bowling masterclass for the ages, perhaps best described by an interested onlooker named Sir Donald Bradman. 'From what I saw that day, Lillee was capable of the most devastation against the best batsmen in the world. The sheer pace he generated opened up weaknesses you wouldn't normally see in such good techniques,' said Bradman, who later named Lillee alongside Alec Bedser and Ray Lindwall in his best ever XI.

> 'From what I saw that day, Lillee was capable of the most devastation against the best batsmen in the world.'

Greg Chappell, who many would rate as Australia's next-best batsman after Bradman, played his entire career alongside Lillee, and thoroughly agrees with Bradman's assessment.

'Dennis Lillee was far and away the best bowler I faced in any grade of cricket. He just kept asking difficult questions. Early on he was up there with the big boys for speed. But he had the change of pace which was the most dangerous ball of all. You were on notice every ball he bowled, which was similar to Malcolm Marshall. They both had such good leg cutters.' Chappell played in that 1971/72 against the Rest of the World and has never forgotten the carnage at the WACA when Lillee steamed in.

Sobers, who didn't face Jeff Thomson at his peak, has always said Lillee's bowling that day was the fastest he ever faced: not as consistently quick as Frank Tyson, but faster in one particular spell.

For the 22-year-old Lillee it was the culmination of some very hard work and a deep desire to win: 'I hated losing in anything, including marbles, which I played a lot of. The same with Monopoly,' says Lillee. 'It was something I was born with, and I was prepared to run myself ragged to achieve. I didn't have a lot of natural ability so I taught myself that if I trained harder than anyone else, I would get there. That was my belief. It was hammered into me by my maternal grandfather, Pop Halifax, who was a boxing coach. He taught me that fitness is number one, and said if your body is fit, then your mind is fit. Once your mind tells you you're tired, then you are.

'I knew early on I was fast, even in the backyard and early on at school. I didn't ever say I was going to be the fastest bowler in the world,

Dennis Lillee

73

it was more a case of being able to naturally bowl fast. I rarely tried an inswinger at all because I was taught that the best ball was an outswinger, particularly when you had three slips and a gully.

'Graham McKenzie was a hero to me, as were Ray Lindwall, Keith Miller, Wes Hall and Alan Davidson before him. I had a lot of faith put in me by my captains, and it allowed me to experiment more as a bowler. Captains such as John Inverarity and Ian Chappell showed a lot of respect for me too, which helped enormously. Sledging was never something I planned, it just sometimes came out of frustration, and normally it was fairly harmless stuff.'

And it was, usually laced with a fair sprinkling of Lillee humour, though there was an occasion at the WACA where the tension threatened to spill over. The fast bowler famously tapped Javed Miandad with his foot, to which Pakistan's agent provocateur responded by raising his bat as if to strike Lillee, prompting umpire Tony Crafter to intervene.

But the real Lillee was more bark than bite, and there was a bubbling humour ready to surface. His Western Australian teammate and future Australian chairman of selectors, John Inverarity, saw the Lillee wit on the 1972 tour of England: 'We were playing Leicester in a tour game and he was really on song. "Garth" [Graham] McKenzie was batting for Leicester and I was at second slip. These kids were playing cricket alongside us and their tennis ball came onto the ground, which Dennis duly picked up and bowled. He bowled it so fast that I thought the inner core had come out. Another time down at Howe, in a muck-around type game, there were these beautiful shining apples at lunch. Naturally Dennis grabbed one and bowled it for the first ball of the match. It hit the pitch and broke into many pieces. Yes, he could also be aggressive, and there were

'I knew early on I was fast, even in the backyard and early on at school.'

John Inverarity
ON LILLEE

'When I first spotted Dennis he was quite slender, and ran in fast and bowled wildly. I played him in a club game early on. There was a lot to cut, short stuff outside the off-stump. When he first bowled for WA he ran in very fast and bowled very fast. Not surprisingly he came through the ranks quickly, and we were aware of him early on.

I remember rooming with him on the train going to Sydney. There was only one bed, the other one being a fold-up, and I told him I was the senior player and said, "You will have to make do in that little bed." He accepted it because he was naive to start with, but he learnt quickly. In fact his learning curve was very steep. His action became more refined as he learnt to run. I remember saying to Ian Brayshaw fairly early that he was better than Garth [Graeme McKenzie], which was a big statement. In those days Dennis bowled every ball as quickly as he could.

The exceptional thing with him was his will. He trained so hard, and I have never seen anyone run to the degree he did. At 4.45pm he was wanting the ball, a joy to captain. Early on he sometimes fell away and pushed it down leg-side. In his first Test match in Adelaide, after the opening day he had just one wicket. He was racing in and falling away and angling the ball in. The next day he settled down, got close to the stumps and moved it away to take five wickets. It was just a matter of getting his technique right.'

Dennis Lillee

> With his left arm high, a steady acceleration to the crease and a fierce follow-through, Lillee developed a textbook action.

plenty of glares and stares – plus a fair degree of fire in the belly and eyes – but Dennis has always had a good sense of fun.'

English captain Mike Brearley, who regards Lillee as the perfect fast bowler, the best he played against, remembers playing a forward defensive push at the WACA that Lillee fielded on his follow-through. Rather than picking up the ball and returning to his mark, Lillee dropped it like a hot coal and started ringing his hand as if the power of Brearley's dribbling drive had caused some serious pain.

At his peak Lillee stood 182cm, or just short of six feet in the old. But he was such a supreme physical specimen, and so tall at the point of delivery, that he appeared a towering presence when motoring to the wicket. With his left arm high, a steady acceleration to the crease and a fierce follow-through, Lillee developed a textbook action. When asked years later about his action, he preferred to speak about Sir Richard Hadlee, Bob Massie and Terry Alderman as three bowlers he felt had totally efficient actions.

Brearley was well placed to road test the dark-haired Australian (whose signature headband was a compulsory accessory for kids of the time).

Dennis Lillee

The Cambridge-educated Englishman was part of a 1977 Centenary Test team at the MCG that won the toss and, under captain Tony Greig, watched Australia capitulate on a green wicket for just 138. With England 1/28 at stumps, and Brearley still at the crease, Greig's smile couldn't be wiped off his face. He claimed in an interview after play that he couldn't have been happier if he lived to ninety-five. Greig's words proved prophetic when, with Lillee bowling to a field that at one stage included six in the slips and gully, England was bowled out for 95.

But as the second day wore on the wicket quietened considerably, allowing Australian captain Greg Chappell to declare at 9/419, setting England 453 for an unlikely victory. Lillee began as his career had begun, full of fire and brimstone, before realising another way would have to be found. So, in what would become cricket's version of the rope-a-dope tactics employed two years earlier by Muhammad Ali against George Foreman, Lillee changed his entire game plan, the famous outswing replaced by inswing and leg cutters on a pitch that increasingly kept low. From 34.4 overs he finished with 5/139, bowling England out for a fighting 417.

Perhaps assessing Lillee is best left to one who is often mentioned alongside him when the greatest bowlers are discussed. Sir Richard Hadlee, who also began his career as an out-and-out paceman before refining his bowling style, couldn't be higher in his praise, once declaring that Lillee was 'my idol, my role model ... I copied Lillee. I studied him and analysed everything he did, asking myself why he did it and whether there were aspects of his approach I could build into my own game.'

HOGGY'S VIEW

THE FIRST TIME I SAW HIM I THINK IT WAS HIS FIRST

Shield game for WA. It was at the MCG and he would have been about nineteen. I was an eighteen-year-old fast bowler in the Victorian State squad, so naturally I took interest in any fellow quick. As I walked up the steps of the old Southern Stand I saw this magnificent sight: a runaway train named Dennis Lillee. It was the best thing I had ever seen. I just thought, *how good is this?*

I first met him in 1975 in the Lion Hotel in Adelaide. I couldn't speak because I was so nervous being next to him, even though he was only a year older than me. To play alongside him a few years later was the biggest honour of my sporting life. To see him go into another zone, to see his will first-hand was something else. He was always so encouraging. Sometimes superstars don't want to pass things on.

> To see him go into another zone, to see his will first-hand was something else.

For tenacity and sheer desire to pull wickets out of nowhere, he is clearly the best. We all rave about the West Indies, but don't worry, he was their inspiration – as he was for just about every fast bowler in the world. There were two stages to Dennis, pre-

1977, after his second injury breakdown, which prevented him going to England, and then the well-oiled robot after that. Don't worry, he loved it most when he could push off the sightscreen to watch the ball thump into the gloves of Rod Marsh. He never lost the thrill of taking Test wickets, but taking them as a bowler who could put the wind up any batsman was his favourite time. That his wickets (24) against the Rest of the World in 1971/72 aren't recognised is a disgrace. That tour was sanctioned by the Australian Cricket Board, so surely it should count.

Dennis Lillee

SIR WES HALL

Born 12 September 1937, Glebe Land,
Station Hill, St Michael, Barbados

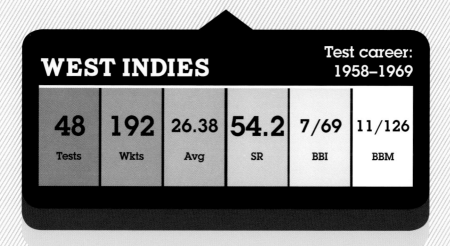

WEST INDIES

Test career:
1958–1969

48	192	26.38	54.2	7/69	11/126
Tests	Wkts	Avg	SR	BBI	BBM

A senator, reverend and more recently a knight, Sir Wesley Winfield Hall remains the archetypal West Indian fast bowler.

HAILING FROM A CARIBBEAN ISLAND NAMED

Barbados, which seemed to have a factory producing tall men who could bowl very fast for long periods, Sir Wes Hall is rightfully regarded as the father of West Indian fast bowling.

A senator, reverend and more recently a knight, Sir Wesley Winfield Hall remains the archetypal West Indian fast bowler: a lengthy run-up that strongly suggested furious pace, arms flailing, ever-present gold crucifix bouncing off his chest as he made his way on a 26-step journey. Yes, there had been pacemen from the Islands before Hall, with Sir Learie Constantine and Roy Gilchrist still spoken of, but Hall was the prototype for what would become cricket's greatest ever arsenal.

This makes it even harder to believe he didn't begin as a tearaway quick. Like others of his craft, with Mike Procter and Malcolm Marshall sharing the same cricketing initiation, Hall began as a batsman/wicketkeeper

Sir Wes Hall

Hall's
BEST BOWLERS

ROY GILCHRIST

'He was only 5'8", but was like a runaway locomotive: a really fearsome bowler. But he was sent home from Pakistan for disciplinary reasons at age twenty-five and never played Test cricket again.'

CHARLIE GRIFFITH

'A big, strong man. People would look for a chink in his armour and they tried to belittle him over his action. I will tell you that compared to some of these fellas I see today, Charlie Griffith was the purest of the pure. What I see today passing for bowlers, they are not bowling. All the doosra bowlers are chuckers, no doubt about that.'

FRED TRUEMAN

'I was a great admirer of Fred Trueman. He had a great side-on action.'

JEFF THOMSON

'I think the quickest I have seen might have been that whirlwind. He was so fast with that slinging action. There was nowhere to hide from him and Dennis Lillee.'

ALAN DAVIDSON

'They don't come better than him.'

FRANK TYSON

'Was called "the Typhoon" and for good reason, because he was so quick it wasn't funny. And then the West Indies had six of them in the early 1980s.'

Sir Wes Hall

HITTING BATSMEN

'Of course I bowled in the days of no helmets, but I can remember the English players getting dressed up like knights in armour or American football gear. There were padded vests, thigh pads, arm guards. I always felt so sorry when I hit a batsman. Colin McDonald was one. You don't want to damage a fella. Today, with their helmets on, they head balls like soccer players. They don't move their feet as well. Bob Simpson: the only time I touched him was when I shook his hand. He was quick-fire. He wouldn't duck, just sway out of the way. He had such a good technique for playing fast bowling. He and his wife, Meg, are beautiful people, and just some of the many Australians I became friends with after the Australian tour. Great rivals on the field, great friends off it. That's how it should be.'

before becoming an accidental fast-bowling hero. He attended the Combermere Secondary School on a scholarship and prided himself as an opening batsman, figuring bowling was for mugs who wanted to toil in the hot sun all day. Soon enough he won promotion to the school senior team where competition for batting spots was fierce, so in the hope he could add an extra string to his bow, Hall read a book titled *Behind the Stumps* by English wicketkeeping great Godfrey Evans.

It was in this guise that Hall remained at school, even keeping wickets in a couple of games against an off spinner named Charlie Griffith, who would later partner Hall in one of cricket's most frightening fast-bowling pairings. And Hall knew all about fast-bowling pairs, having witnessed the carnage dished out by Australians Ray Lindwall and Keith Miller on their West Indies tour of 1955.

Sir Wes Hall

In many ways Hall would emulate Miller a decade later. Both were showmen who could draw people through the turnstiles, both cricketers who were loved wherever they travelled. If Bradman drew crowds through sheer weight of runs, Hall and Miller did the same by being genuinely entertaining and always respecting opponents.

The revered West Indian statesman and cricket captain Sir Frank Worrell was asked to pen some words for Hall's 1966 autobiography, *Pace Like Fire*. Of Hall he wrote: 'Wes Hall may impress other fast bowlers that one can succeed without displaying general hatred and abuse of the batsman … Wes is one of the few who can take his licks like a man. There is not the least trace of egotism in the man and unlike most fast bowlers he discusses cricket in any terms except the first-person singular.'

> 'There is not the least trace of egotism in the man and unlike most fast bowlers he discusses cricket in any terms except the first-person singular.'

Worrell knew how lucky his cricket team had been to have stumbled across someone who would lead the country's pace attack for ten years, a decade in which Hall didn't miss a Test. This was in a period (from 1962 to 1967) where the West Indies were undefeated in any series, winning fifteen Tests and losing just three, long before Clive Lloyd and Sir Vivian Richards led the all-conquering sides between 1976 and 1990.

As a teenager Hall would occasionally bowl in the nets, sometimes imagining he was one of the Aussies but never thinking it would lead to anything. Then came one of those moments that changes the fortunes of a nation. As Hall was buckling up his pads, to either open the batting or keep for the Bridgetown Cable Office against another Barbados team, his captain asked if he would mind opening the bowling, given the absence of their usual quick. Six wickets later

Sir Wes Hall

a career was born, Hall touring England shortly afterwards despite having just one first-class game to his name.

'Back then I didn't know very much about bowling at all and was really never coached. I was a bit wild but had quite a good action and I could always bowl a big outswinger. Everton Weekes was someone who encouraged me when I was named in the twenty-six for two trial games, before the touring party for England in 1957 was announced,' says Hall.

'Everton said, "I can help you with your bowling in the field, but not your batting." I didn't do well in the first trial but in the second game I bowled as well as could be expected before scoring 41 and 77, and by the end of the match I was in the touring party, even though I had been bowling for less than a year.'

Hall didn't play a Test in England but started to understand what was required to become a feared fast bowler like his little mate Roy Gilchrist. He ran and ran, strengthening his body, and bowled for hours at a single stump. By the time he was picked to tour India in 1958/59, he was ready for his Test debut.

'I was about the fifth bowler selected in that side after Frank Worrell had to withdraw, and I had no real hope of getting a Test. But Roy Gilchrist was my roommate and really helped get me in the side. I did well in the tour game and got in for the first Test, then ended up with 30 wickets in five matches and we won the series. Then we went to Pakistan where I got 16 wickets in three Tests, so I came back with 46 wickets in eight Tests. My speed was very good, almost up to Gilchrist, who was the fastest bowler in the world at that time.'

> He ran and ran, strengthening his body, and bowled for hours at a single stump.

Sir Wes Hall

Wes Hall bowling to Tom Graveney, The Oval, London, 1966.

Sir Wes Hall

The most famous of Hall's Tests took place in Australia on a 1960/61 tour. The Aussies won the five-match series 2/1, yet either side could have emerged victorious and cricket still would have been the overall winner. And a big part of that tour's success was the 191cm frame of Hall putting everything into every ball he bowled, or the '50 per cent inspiration and 50 per cent perspiration' that Hall believes any great fast bowler requires for success.

Hall captured the bonhomie of the Caribbean, a much-loved man who has close friendships with many of his opponents. For the early part of his career he was forced to work without the bonus of a genuine opening partner, something he believed was strongly to his detriment.

'A lot of the great fast bowlers, Ray Lindwall and Keith Miller, Fred Trueman and Brian Statham, have been pairings. It doesn't give batsmen the chance to sit on you and not take any chances by playing strokes. What they would tend to do is take risks at the other end. I opened early on with medium pacers Garry Sobers and Frank Worrell, who were great bowlers in their own rights but first change options,' says Hall. 'It was a great pity Roy Gilchrist and Charlie Griffith didn't go to Australia in 1960/61. I bowled at 95m/h [approx. 152km/h] at one end with Sir Frank Worrell and Garry Sobers at 75–80m/h [approx. 120–128km/h] at the other end. So there was pace at only one end. The Test series might have been different, and even better, with Gilchrist and Griffith playing.'

> Hall captured the bonhomie of the Caribbean, a much-loved man who has close friendships with many of his opponents.

When the West Indies toured Australia in 1960/61, Hall, Sobers and Worrell made up the attack against Australian openers Colin McDonald and Bob Simpson. That summer is still regarded by many as the pinnacle of Test match cricket. It captured everything the game prides itself on: exhilarating

1960/61 TOUR OF AUSTRALIA

'I will never forget Collins Street in Melbourne after the fifth Test. They said there were 500,000 people there, yelling out, "Come back soon." I remember an article by Keith Miller saying a series like that could never happen again, and he was right. The feeling between the two teams was so healthy. The young and the old, streamers everywhere, it was a true reflection of how the cricket was played. We had gone to Australia as a group of good cricketers, but had never really gelled as a team as such because we were from different islands, different religions, different cultures. It took a great man like Frank Worrell to bring us together. We became world champions after that, well before Clive Lloyd and Viv Richards in the 1976–1990 period.'

batting, lightning slips catching, almost unimaginable outfielding, attacking captaincy, faultless sportsmanship and breathtaking fast bowling from Hall.

McDonald and Simpson faced that bowling with some skill, combining for 782 runs in a pre-helmet era. Hall has never forgotten McDonald's courage: 'Colin McDonald would have to be one of the most courageous batsmen I bowled to. Brian Close from England was another. I can remember striking McDonald on the upper body and he fell to his knees. I ran straight down to see how he was and to apologise, but before I could speak he said, "No, it was my fault." I struck him several times around the ribs but he never complained once.'

Sir Wes Hall

Wes Hall (bottom row, second from the left) and the West Indian cricket team, 1966.

McDonald chuckles when recalling Hall's words, well remembering the incident. 'By the time they came in 1960 the whole world knew Wes Hall was a very fast bowler, and he didn't disappoint us. The first time I faced Hall was in Perth, in an invitational team prior to the first Test. In those days there were no Tests in Perth, so what they would do was send three or four eastern state Test players to bolster the Western Australian team. Don Bradman was watching in his role as a selector, and after I got a few runs against Hall he said, "Colin, that is the fastest bowling I have ever seen", which I thought wasn't bad given he had played against Harold Larwood in the 1932/33 Bodyline series.

'It was nice of Wes Hall to say I was courageous, but when I was spread-eagled on the Gabba pitch, if I wasn't showing pain then I don't know what his definition of pain was. He didn't overuse the short ball because he quickly realised it was useless bowling a ball that went three to four feet over your head. But he played the game in absolutely the proper way, as did all of his teammates, led by a fine person in Frank Worrell. And for sheer speed Wes Hall was the quickest, just ahead of Tyson. Then there was the South African pair in Peter Heine and Neil Adcock, plus Keith Miller on his day and of course the great Ray Lindwall.'

Sir Wes Hall

> ## 'He was very, very quick but over-bowled.'

Hall's wish for a fast-bowling partner was answered in the brooding form of Charlie Griffith, a fellow Barbadian who burst on the scene in the early 1960s. Bob Simpson faced Hall in both Australia (1960/61), and when Hall worked in tandem with Griffith in the West Indies (1965). What Hall lacked in natural aggression was made up for by Griffith, a quietly spoken man who during that tour was largely unknown to the Australians. Griffith had been called for throwing in the past, so it was natural for him to view the cricketing world with a certain lack of trust, but the Australians who got to know him later found him good company. Still, with a ball in his hand he was far from anyone's friend.

'I had faced Wes before, in 1960/61,' says Simpson. 'He was very lively then, quicker than he was in the West Indies in 1965. He was very, very quick but over-bowled, and by the end of the tour he was tired. He was the quickest I faced and we hadn't struck that pace, so early on he could make it uncomfortable. He had what I would call a pure action, making it easier to follow his movements.

'Griffith wasn't as pure as Wes Hall, but in some ways could be even more dangerous because he would fall away dramatically at the point of delivery. He used to be really nasty when he got going. I ended up taking off-stump to him because he was always coming into you, like Colin Croft. The more you face a fast bowler, the easier they become, which was apparent in the West Indies on that 1965 tour, because as the season wore on we got more runs against them. The big problem is if you haven't seen them before.

'There was no carry-on from Wes like you sometimes see today. I faced Frank Tyson when I was nineteen, but I always say Wesley Hall is the fastest I faced.'

Sir Wes Hall

Hall's
BEST BATSMEN

KEN BARRINGTON

'Not as pleasing to the eye as Peter May, Colin Cowdrey and Tom Graveney, but he was the hardest to get out.'

TED DEXTER

'You didn't want Dexter to bat three hours against you because he would punish you.'

SIR CONRAD HUNTE

'A beautiful player but suffered from not having a solid partner, meaning he had to change his style. We also had Frank Worrell, Garry Sobers, Rohan Kanhai and Seymour Nurse. It was a great era for batsmen.'

TOM GRAVENEY

'Very early on in my career Tom Graveney got a hundred. I bowled a short ball to him and he nonchalantly hooked it over the scoreboard. He came down to me and said, "Don't worry lad, you are a good bowler and you will be alright, but I'm on the go so don't worry what I do." Three years later in England I bowled him two bounces and had him on the ground, and I said, "Come on, get up, you are a great little player but I am on the go." We had a good laugh.'

SIR GARRY SOBERS AND OTHERS

'Sir Garry was something else as a cricketer, but as a batsman he was just brilliant. Bob Simpson was also a fantastic player. So were Colin McDonald, Neil Harvey and Norman O'Neill. Peter Burge was very talented.'

HOGGY'S VIEW

SIR WES HALL WAS THE REASON I WANTED TO BE A fast bowler. I watched the West Indies play Victoria on that 1960/61 tour at the MCG when Rohan Kanhai got one of the great first-class double centuries. After watching Wes Hall bowl, and bat for that matter, I told my dad that was who I was going to become. He explained I was the wrong colour and wasn't going to be tall enough, but it didn't stop me. I would make Dad and the kid from next door, who hated cricket, face me while I tried to knock their blocks off. I also loved the way Wes batted. He wasn't Sir Garry Sobers, but he was a genuine entertainer. The crowds seriously loved him. He got 50-odd on that tour at the MCG, and every run was wildly clapped. When he bowled it seemed like he left nothing on the park.

> After watching Wes Hall bowl, and bat for that matter, I told my dad that was who I was going to become.

Sir Wes Hall

MIKE PROCTER

'Procky'

Born 15 September 1946,
Durban, Natal

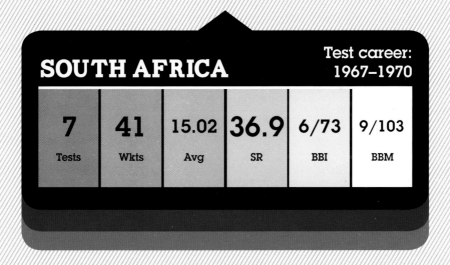

SOUTH AFRICA				Test career: 1967–1970	
7	**41**	15.02	**36.9**	6/73	9/103
Tests	Wkts	Avg	SR	BBI	BBM

There has never been a cricket coach worth their salt who could point to Procter's action as one to copy.

MIKE PROCTER, HE OF THE DEPRIVED CRICKETING
life, was unlike any other: a brute of a man who relied on a 27-pace run-up to generate fearsome speed and a late swing from a very quick arm action.

There has never been a cricket coach worth their salt who could point to Procter's action as one to copy. There were none of the fluid motions of Michael Holding or the high side-on action of Dennis Lillee, just a self-taught compilation of minimal aesthetics but wonderful results. None of it seemed to fit together easily – the pieces almost worked in opposition – but when the ball was delivered something clicked.

So all the more remarkable that he began his career as a wicketkeeper/batsman, a position many batsmen must wish he had kept. As a schoolboy he was already looked upon as a future Test player, blasting five centuries at age twelve for Highbury Preparatory School, including an undefeated 210. It wasn't until his fifteenth year, at net practice for the first team at Hilton College, that Procter was thrown the ball.

At the time Procter was also highly proficient at rugby union as a fly-half, at hockey for Natal Schools, and at squash, tennis and athletics.

Mike Procter

HITTING BATSMEN

'The bouncer was a part of my game, though obviously I didn't want to hit someone. But of course you must use it as part of your armoury. I did hit a lot of blokes on the head. I hit Barry Richards once on the head, and he had to go to hospital. Another time when we were playing in the Currie Cup, I hit the nightwatchman. It was very serious because he ended up in hospital for ten days. He came in as a nightwatchman, but in club cricket he was an opening batsman. I bowled a bouncer which smashed him on the cheek, and it just wasn't very nice, not something you would ever plan to do or want to happen.'

But it was cricket – bred into him by his father, Woodrow, who had played at first-class level in South Africa – where Procter's passions lay.

His career coincided with that of another prodigy, the ever-correct opening batsman Barry Richards. In 1965 an enterprising English county named Gloucestershire, home of men such as Dr WG Grace, Wally Hammond and Tom Graveney, enticed Procter and Richards over for trials. At Gloucestershire the pair played in the second team until the arrival of Peter van der Merwe's touring South Africans. Procter and Richards were promoted to play against their countrymen and, with a pair of 60s, proved that they belonged. Those at Gloucestershire never forgot Procter, and it became his county home from 1968–81, often referred to as 'Proctershire', such was his influence with bat and ball. By the end his body no longer allowed him the 'bull at a gate' approach, and at times he bowled off-spin – and with success.

Mike Procter

But early on, before South Africa was ostracised from Test cricket due to its racist apartheid policy, Procter was given a brief chance to display his talents on a world stage. Thanks to two strong South African sides, his batting wasn't required as much as his ability, with teammate Peter Pollock, to produce an opening attack that could blast the Australians out. Most great cricketing nations have built their success on a fast-bowling duo, whether it be Ray Lindwall and Keith Miller, Dennis Lillee and Jeff Thomson, or Wasim Akram and Waqar Younis. The Pollock and Procter team sits comfortably among these, even if they were reduced to just seven Tests.

> '**I worked out that with my quick arm action, the longer I ran in, the quicker I bowled.**'

They first played in the third Test of the 1966/67 South Africa–Australia series, when the home side won 3/1, and a young Procter announced himself with seven wickets in the match, which his team won by eight wickets. In fact Procter would never play in a losing Test, and his record stands at six wins and a draw against the hapless Australians. 'In that first series I was just twenty and it was all very new when you were bowling to players such as Bob Simpson, Bill Lawry, Bob Cowper, Ian Chappell, Keith Stackpole and Ian Redpath,' recalls Procter.

'I started as a batsman who kept wicket. At age fifteen I was small, but they needed an opening bowler, so while I wasn't quick I gave it a go. Just over four years later I was opening the bowling to the Australians. I worked out that with my quick arm action, the longer I ran in, the quicker I bowled. I didn't have a side-on action, it was all arm and movement. By seventeen to eighteen I became quicker and quicker but was very much a late developer.

'What I could always do was swing the ball and I think I was always okay at actually getting a batsman out. In my second Test at the

Mike Procter

Procter's
BEST BOWLERS

JEFF THOMSON AND DENNIS LILLEE

'Renowned, and for a very good reason. They were so formidable.'

MIKEY HOLDING

'Possibly the fastest of the West Indians from that great period in the 1970s–80s–90s. He always allowed you to see the ball in his run-up, but you still had to deal with his pace.'

SYLVESTER CLARKE

'The most underrated fast bowler of all time. He bowled a very heavy ball and really accelerated off the pitch. He should have played Test cricket for fifteen years.'

JOEL GARNER

'Had a fantastic yorker and bouncer and was quick enough.'

PETER HEINE AND NEIL ADCOCK

'Formidable South African quicks.'

DALE STEYN

'A magnificent bowler. He can't be described as fast in comparison to some of those a generation or so before, but he would have been a very good bowler in any era.'

Mike Procter

Wanderers Stadium in Johannesburg we were trying to get quick wickets in Australia's second innings on the third night because we knew there was rain coming. I was bowling over the wicket to Bill Lawry, who was a magnificent player of both pace and spin. I went around the wicket knowing that Bill, a left-hander, would be expecting the ball to swing away from him. So I held the ball across the seam. Bill began to play before leaving it, and the ball ended up clipping his off-stump.'

'He was quick and awkward with that unusual sort of half back-foot action.'

By the time the Australians returned in 1970, Procter was an even more imposing figure, his body match-hardened after a couple of seasons in both Currie Cup and English County level. Doug Walters, a batsman as natural as any to play for his country, had missed Procter in 1967 due to national service for the Vietnam War, but he had heard all about him from his teammates.

'He was quick and awkward with that unusual sort of half back-foot action. I would describe him as very slippery back in those days, and he gave you a fair bit of short stuff. Apart from Cape Town he bowled on seaming wickets on our 1970 tour,' recalls Walters.

'He was an extremely good bowler and an extremely good cricketer. If you get around 50 first-class centuries and have a bowling average of under 20 then you are going alright. In terms of pace, those West Indies guys in Andy Roberts, Michael Holding, Joel Garner and Colin Croft, I reckon they were all the same pace, all quick, but I couldn't say one was quicker than the other. I would put John Snow and Mike Procter into that same category, plus Dennis Lillee early on.'

Keith Stackpole was present at all of Procter's seven Tests: 'Because he wasn't a tall fellow he didn't get that much bounce, so he was what

Mike Procter

Mike Procter and Gloucestershire captain Tony Brown are carried by their team after victory over Sussex in the Gillette Cup Final. Lord's, London, 1973.

I would classify as a skidding bowler. When he started he was mainly an inswinger but later on he developed the one that went away a little bit,' recalls Stackpole.

'He was similar to Maxie Walker, but much quicker. He was genuinely sharp, someone who pitched it up more than bowled short. He was well-disciplined as a bowler and potentially one of the world's greatest all-rounders. The only reason we don't speak of him that way is because he didn't play more Test cricket. A really good guy, fairly quiet and a lot less demonstrative than they are today. In terms of speed think of Ryan Harris, but about five kilometres faster.'

Paul Sheahan was a teammate of Stackpole and Walters on that 1970 tour: 'Procky was so quick bowling inswingers that he always cramped you for room. On tracks that were prepared to suit their pace attack, he was outstanding. By the time he got to the crease he was actually sprinting. Because of his unorthodox run-up he seemed to need to generate most of his speed through his run-up. Because he was front-on he didn't get much out of his shoulders and body.

Mike Procter

'I faced Dennis Lillee and Jeff Thomson in Shield cricket, and outside of the Australians "Procky" was the quickest. And because he did something with it he was even harder to face. He was so dangerous because he moved the ball substantially in the air at pace. You had to get your feet moving and try not to be predictable because he quickly realised what you were doing and he would adjust.'

But by the time Sheahan and the Australians departed South Africa in 1970, Procter's Test career was over due to the South African government's appalling apartheid, a system that refused to treat the black population as equal citizens. Far from being embittered, Procter believes in some ways he was lucky.

'I look at Jacques Kallis, who was a once-in-a-lifetime cricketer, but he never got to see the world's greatest leader, Nelson Mandela, come through the most terrible adversity to rise to power. Mandela became my ultimate hero. I witnessed the challenges he faced through the apartheid years, and ultimately his nation-building powers, which saved our country. I wouldn't trade that for anything.

'So I don't feel robbed. If it's between me missing one Test and changing the lives of forty million people, then that is fine. I knew I wasn't going to play Test cricket after two tours were cancelled so I was able to get my head around that. Of course there are times I think I could have played a lot more Tests and done okay, but in my heart of hearts I knew what was happening in South Africa was totally wrong, so I didn't feel that bad about it.

Mike Procter

'It made playing County cricket for Gloucestershire that much more special. And in 1970 I played in a Rest of the World side with men like Garry Sobers, Rohan Kanhai, Lance Gibbs, Clive Lloyd, Farokh Engineer and Intikhab Alam. We beat Ray Illingworth's English side 3/1, with Illingworth's side then beating Australia in Australia. I still can't believe it wasn't classified as Test cricket.'

From then until World Series Cricket broke out seven years later, Procter performed regular miracles in both County cricket and South Africa's domestic competition, the Currie Cup. You only need to visit YouTube to witness one of his finest, a 1977 Benson and Hedges 50-over Cup semi-final against a Hampshire line-up that included Barry Richards and Gordon Greenidge. Four wickets in five balls and match figures of 6/13 led to an unlikely win before setting up for victory in the final. Two years later he was at it again, this time against the touring Indians.

'The semi-final against Hampshire was on a flat deck in Southampton, and our score of 195 was below par. Richards and Greenidge opened the batting and looked pretty solid so I decided to bowl around the wicket. It started to swing so I pitched it up, then got Barry and Gordon out and a hat-trick. We ended up winning the final to give us our second bit of silverware [including the 1973 Gillette Cup] since the days of WG Grace. When Gloucestershire played India in 1979 it was important for me, because I couldn't play Test cricket and anytime you got to test yourself against the best was like a Test.

'In terms of speed think of Ryan Harris, but about five kilometres faster.'

'The Indians had Sunny Gavaskar, Gundappa Viswanath, Dilip Vengsarkar, Mohinder Amarnath and Kapil Dev in their batting line-up, so they had some serious class. They batted and declared at 5/337, then we replied with 7/254. I then took 7/13 off 15 overs to set up a seven-wicket win, so that was extremely satisfying.'

Mike Procter

Procter's
BEST BATSMEN

BARRY RICHARDS

'So technically good that it made it hard to pinpoint a weakness, and he could score fluently without seeming to rush.'

GEOFF BOYCOTT

'Someone I always found hard to get out, he did have a very good defence.'

SIR GARRY SOBERS

'Could play any shot on any side of the wicket, a total natural.'

GRAEME POLLOCK

'Blessed with wonderful concentration and obvious timing. He found the gaps and scored at every opportunity with ease.'

SIR VIV RICHARDS

'Could slaughter you. He could hit the ball from any position to wherever he wanted, the strongest leg-side player I have seen.'

SUNIL GAVASKAR

'So straight, in that he presented the full face of the bat.'

Mike Procter

HOGGY'S VIEW

I SHOULD BEGIN BY SAYING THAT 'PROCKY', AS HE'S known, is one of the most delightful men you could meet in world cricket, respected everywhere for his gracious and modest manner. Sadly that is where the pleasantries end, for I was amazed to learn he took not even the smallest bit of joy in really scaring batsmen. Cleary Mike Procter doesn't belong in the lunatic room for fast bowlers such as myself, probably because he is both too smart and just too good a bloke.

How do I rate him as a cricketer? Behind Sir Garry Sobers, he would be in a group with Jacques Kallis, Keith Miller and Imran Khan as one of the best all-rounders the game has seen. I detest the fact that Test cricket was robbed of his talents for so long. Then again it meant I never had to face him, and as a self-confessed coward that suited me fine. His action was so unusual, like a faster version of Max Walker and Lance Cairns. And like those two he had a magnificent inswinger and the ability to go around the wicket and bring the ball back into the right-handers, which opened up LBW and bowled, such as in that One Day game against Hampshire in 1977.

Mike Procter

BRETT LEE

'Binga'

Born 8 November 1976,
Wollongong, New South Wales

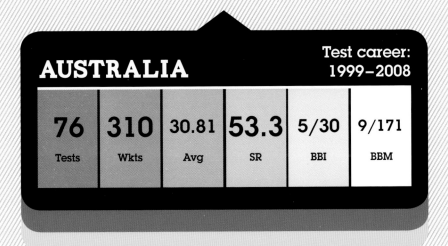

AUSTRALIA				Test career: 1999–2008	
76	**310**	30.81	**53.3**	5/30	9/171
Tests	Wkts	Avg	SR	BBI	BBM

For Lee to see the speed gun hit 160km/h was the culmination of a childhood dream.

WITH ARMS THAT PUMPED LIKE THE PISTONS
of a well-oiled V8, a running style akin to that of an Olympic sprinter and an approach to the wicket that was a perfect example of increasing momentum, Brett Lee could have been the poster boy for any fast-bowling manual. His action was poetry in motion, all the parts coming together to create the kind of extreme pace that few have ever achieved in Australian cricket history – arguably, only Jeff Thomson or Shaun Tait could ever have surpassed it.

For Lee to see the speed gun hit 160km/h was the culmination of a childhood dream, one that had begun at age nine when he told his parents he wanted to do two things: grow taller, and become the fastest bowler in the world.

And because of his extreme athleticism he was able to sustain his speed for healthy periods, as highlighted when it all came together in 2005 during a One Day game of historic proportions. The venue was McLean Park in New Zealand's seaside city of Napier, the date, 5 March. Lee's figures, a somewhat uninspiring 1/34, show little of what was one of the most withering displays of sustained pace ever seen. It began in his first

THE FAST BOWLER'S BODY

'I worked hard on my body, but I was never a big gym fan. I tried to stay slim and keep my core strength. Some guys do too many weights, and it doesn't make them bowl quicker – Dale Steyn is almost perfect in build. My quickest spell was either in 1999 in the Shield game at the WACA where I broke Joe Angel's arm, or in 2005. A week after that Shield game I took 5/47 against India at the MCG in my first Test and bowled at 157km/h, but it felt a lot slower than the Shield game. Then in 2005 I bowled 160.8km/h in New Zealand, and from 2003 to 2006 was my golden era. I was 85 kilograms in 2005, and I wasn't that muscly but I was whippy. I wouldn't recommend too many weights to a young bloke coming through. I did it towards the end of my career to try and show the selectors I was having a crack. I put five kilos on but ended up feeling better when I lost three again.'

over, a consummate display of the art of sheer pace combined with a sharp outswing that made the job of New Zealand's opening batsmen, Craig Cumming and Stephen Fleming, near impossible.

His opening over kicked off with a rather sedate 143km/h before he unleashed all hell and let fly to the tune of 151km/h, 158km/h, 158km/h, 160km/h and then 160.8km/h. YouTube footage of his action shows an easy approach that belies the terror he delivered.

Cumming describes it as quicker than what he faced from Shoaib Akhtar. 'You just see the ball and ask your mind to make a decision. If you make the wrong decision, you pay,' he says.

Brett Lee

Lee's
BEST BOWLERS

SHOAIB AKHTAR

'Probably the fastest. He was absolutely rapid, and you just had to watch the ball so closely.'

SHAUN TAIT

'For sheer speed, Shaun, who I faced over twelve or thirteen years, would also be right up there. It was hard to pick up the ball because of his action. The same with Shoaib, because they both threw their bowling hand behind their back just before delivery. I think if you asked batsmen, they would say I was easier to pick up because my action was more normal. But that doesn't necessarily help if the ball is coming at you around 155km/h.'

DEVON MALCOLM

'Bowled very fast and was still doing it at forty.'

MITCHELL JOHNSON

'Has more of a classic action, but he totally refined the way he played in terms of his ability to bowl aggressively. He was on the outer then worked on his fitness and threw caution to the wind by just bowling fast, plus he is more confident.'

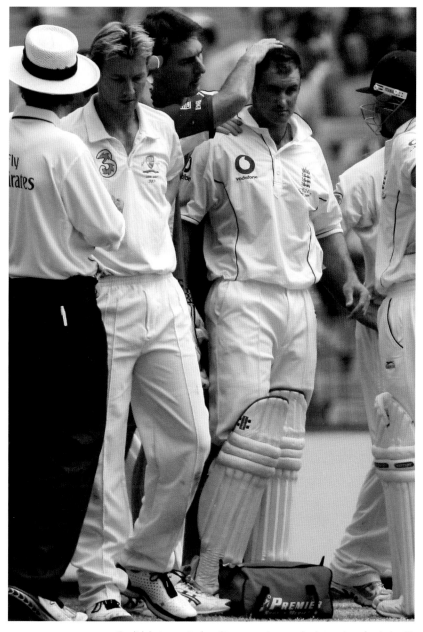

English batsman Andrew Strauss receives medical attention after being hit on the helmet by a Brett Lee delivery. SCG, Sydney, 2007.

Brett Lee

> It's possible Lee never bowled consistently faster, or with more rhythm and venom than that day in Napier.

These sentiments are backed up by Fleming, who describes Lee's bowling as something that left you with 'hangovers and headaches'. Fleming will never forget seeing Lee's 160.8km/h ball flash up on the screen as 161km/h. 'Bowlers talk about seeing their speeds, but don't worry, batsmen take notice of them as well. On that occasion it was impossible not to, because it was flashing like a beacon as the word spread all around the ground. Sometimes I think those speed guns can get it wrong but they definitely didn't that day. I was on edge, twitchy if you like. In fact I will make it plainer, I was shitting myself. It became a matter of self-preservation, and I remember thinking, *if he is on target and I get it wrong then I could be in serious trouble.* His action was more traditional than, say, Shoaib Akhtar or Shaun Tait, and you did get a good look at the ball, but at 160km/h it doesn't really matter that much. I had great respect for Brett Lee, the way he presented himself in such a fit condition which allowed him to maintain his pace. Shoaib was just as quick but for shorter periods.'

It's possible Lee never bowled consistently faster, or with more rhythm and venom than that day in Napier. And it came from an action that was largely self-taught, as Lee explains: 'When I was nine my older brother, Shane, came home and wanted to play cricket. He wanted to bat so he threw me the ball, and that was the day I fell in love with the art of fast bowling. I just ran in with basically the same action I had for my whole career. I knew I couldn't bat and I knew I couldn't bowl spin, but bowling fast and hitting the stumps hard was the greatest thing ever. By age thirteen I used to watch the great Dennis Lillee and Thommo [Jeff Thomson], and in particular Allan Donald, who I thought had a beautiful action. He was quick and wore a white sweatband, so I did the same thing because he was my hero. At sixteen I met Dennis

Brett Lee

Lillee for the first time. I had a stress fracture in my lower back, so I was having to tinker with my action to ensure that I would never get injured again. He gave me some good advice.

'I didn't ever get to see Thommo bowl live because we lived about ninety minutes from Sydney and I was usually out playing cricket in the backyard with my brothers. But I have watched a lot of tapes of him and think he probably had the perfect fast-bowling action. That's why it's surprising we haven't seen many try to bowl like him. Maybe it's just too hard to do, and you have to be an exceptional athlete like Jeff Thomson. His action is like an unwound coil, spitting the ball out from behind his back.'

'He was a magnificent specimen and set a really good example.'

Australian batsman Greg Blewett has no doubt where Lee sits in the world of speed: 'He and Akhtar were the quickest. He was more consistent than Shoaib, and while he was probably easier to pick up out of the hand, he had a better bouncer. And Brett got better as his career went on, given that early on he was just a real tearaway with two basic lengths: short or full. He was intimidating, with his big strong run-up, and while not big on sledging he would let you know you were in the contest. I would try and hook or pull when the ball was short and it didn't matter what the wicket was doing or the stage of the game. Occasionally you would get one that was just too quick, and that could be Brett or Shoaib. Brett could bowl longer spells than Shoaib. He was a magnificent specimen and set a really good example to the younger players.'

When reflecting on his career Lee nominates a somewhat obscure 2003 Test in Trinidad as one of his favourite bowling memories. He took four wickets at the Queen's Park Oval in the first innings and

Lee's
BEST BATSMEN

SACHIN TENDULKAR AND BRIAN LARA

'They both seemed to know their games so well, and in Tendulkar's case he eliminated his get-out shots. Both of them wouldn't hook me until they had got themselves in. We looked for weaknesses in them both, and for a moment you thought you might have found one, then the next two balls in that area would be fours.'

VVS LAXMAN

'Would take a 155km/h ball from off-stump and work you behind square. It highlighted what a serious eye he had, and he always seemed to have plenty of time. Other players get hit on the pad before they can get their bat down.'

MARK WAUGH

'In the nets he had so much time it was scary.'

RICKY PONTING

'Could hook me the easiest. Bowlers like Mitch Johnson and me would get brand new balls to bowl with in the nets so we could replicate match situations. "Punter" was the one who always wanted to face us – and you have to remember you have less time in the nets. He would hook us off his nose for fun. He just picked the short ball up so quickly.'

CHRIS CAIRNS

'I always thought Cairns was underrated because he had such a good eye. And he had the confidence to have a crack at you.'

Brett Lee

just one tail-end scalp in the second, but the memory of bowling to a red-hot Brian Lara remains very clear. 'It was hot, very hot, and Brian was at his best. He'd got 91 in the first innings off not many balls, and we had declared in our second innings, setting them around 400. Their only hope was Lara and he got to 90, as only he could. I bowled a long spell to him and bowled quickly – around 155km/h – and managed to keep him in his 90s for what seemed like an hour. He got his century and I didn't get him out, but after we won the game he said that battle between us was one of his most exciting times on the field. I was so locked into that one-on-one battle,' recalls Lee.

When on 94, Lara received a screaming bouncer that prompted him to take both feet from the ground and fling his head back as the ball narrowly missed his helmet. The delivery was perfectly summed up in the commentator's box by the late David Hookes: 'Great bowling, excellent bowling. That has gone past his nose and the Kookaburra has laughed on the way through. A brilliant piece of bowling on a dead fifth-day track against arguably the best player in the world.'

Brett Lee helps Sri Lankan batsman Dilruwan Perera to his feet after they collided mid-pitch. MCG, Melbourne, 2008.

Brett Lee

HITTING BATSMEN

'I was only eleven. I still remember the guy's name, a young bloke called Wesley Croft. We were trying out for a competition when my coach asked me to run in and try to bowl him a bouncer to see if he could play the short ball. He wasn't wearing a helmet, and I can still remember the ball hitting him straight in the mouth, knocking out two or three of his front teeth. There was blood everywhere, I felt sick and went home crying. Mum and Dad took me to the hospital where we offered to pay all of the dental bills, but his father, to his credit, said it was his son's fault because he wasn't wearing a helmet. It really sickened me, and I didn't want to play cricket after that for six months.

After the passing of Phillip Hughes it brought to light how dangerous it is to face a cricket ball. I have bounced so many players. When I was fifteen I was trying out for the Campbelltown first-grade team. There was a guy called Troy Crossland, their captain. I bounced him and broke his jaw in three places, and he was out for six months. It was horrific.

When you're on TV running in fast you look like this big, tough fast bowler, but you don't want to ever see people get hurt. There is nothing wrong with intimidating a batsman to try and stir him up, but you don't want to see blood or injuries. I have probably hit a couple of hundred people in my career, and thank god I didn't hit anyone in the wrong spot.

At first Shane Warne wasn't happy when I hit him at Lord's with a full toss, but he's okay now. I had double cramp in both hamstrings, and really shouldn't have bowled the ball.'

Brett Lee

HOGGY'S VIEW

THE MORE I SAW OF BRETT LEE THE MORE IMPRESSED
I became. You have to have experienced bowling at that level to fully understand just what a magnificent physical specimen Brett was. I remember watching him bowl 10 overs straight in searing heat one day in Adelaide, and I was thinking, *how in the hell did he do that?* The point being he didn't drop his pace. He fitted in so well with Glenn McGrath and Shane Warne, the strike bowler who used to frighten the hell out of batsmen. And he did that because he seemed to possess a short ball with a radar that could target helmets.

When he first came on the scene I wondered whether he could develop the tricks that would allow him to continue when his pace dropped. But he didn't ever need to, because his pace never dropped. Name another fast bowler in history who could reach 150km/h at age thirty-eight? The only one I can think of is Devon Malcolm. All the champs, bowlers like Dennis Lillee, develop a leg cutter or something similar that maintains their strike rate. Brett Lee just kept bowling fast outswingers, and a really good slower ball for the shorter forms of the game. Right up to his last ball for the Sydney Sixers he still had enough pace to keep a batsman from charging him.

Brett Lee

I remember watching him bowl 10 overs straight in searing heat one day in Adelaide, and I was thinking, *how in the hell did he do that?*

The best Australian fast bowler I have seen is Lillee, but if I could come back as someone it would probably be Brett Lee. He was so marketable, and he was fast. Even that greyhound they named after him was super quick. When I buy my first speed boat I'm going to name it 'Binga' after Brett. In fact I can't think of a knock on him … except maybe that chainsaw thing he used to do after taking a wicket – but then I found out he was being paid to do it by an Indian firm, so it made sense. Can't knock a bloke for earning an extra dollar: I would have attempted to fly if there was a quid in it.

Brett Lee

SHANE BOND

'James Bond'

Born 7 June 1975,
Christchurch, Canterbury

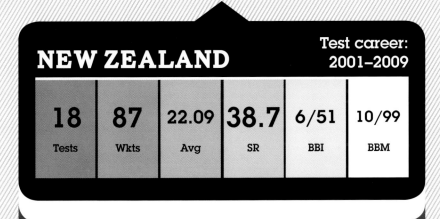

NEW ZEALAND				Test career: 2001–2009	
18	**87**	22.09	**38.7**	6/51	10/99
Tests	Wkts	Avg	SR	BBI	BBM

And it wasn't as if Bond had much of a history, coming from an injury-ridden career with Canterbury in New Zealand's domestic cricket that had shown glimpses of genuine pace.

SHANE BOND WAS NATURALLY FULL OF NERVES ON his Test debut. Bad enough the worries about whether he was up to scratch, let alone bowling to one of the finest batting line-ups ever assembled.

A top seven of Matthew Hayden, Justin Langer, Ricky Ponting, Mark Waugh, Steve Waugh, Damien Martyn and Adam Gilchrist was the stuff of nightmares for any young paceman trying to make his mark on world cricket.

And it wasn't as if Bond had much of a history, coming from an injury-ridden career with Canterbury in New Zealand's domestic cricket that had shown glimpses of genuine pace. At twenty-six, when he measured out his run-up to bowl at Bellerive Oval in Hobart, the Australians were 0/49 when he readied himself to bowl to Langer. The ball was shortish, with Langer shaping to pull before withdrawing from the shot as Bond's extra pace saw it strike the left-hander high on his left arm. It was a sign that he had a bit more – not that the Australian batsmen were too worried, given Hayden blasted 91, and Langer and Ponting scored tons.

QUICKEST SPELL

'There was a Test at Eden Park in Auckland where we were defending 290 against the West Indies and they reached 1/150-odd with a batting line-up that included Gayle, Lara, Sarwan and Chanderpaul. I hit Sarwan with a short ball which was a nasty one and bowled Lara around his legs. Then the ball started to reverse and I ended up with five in a match that we ended up winning by 27 runs. It was an innings when I got players out the way that I wanted to, which doesn't always happen. A few years before that I had bowled pretty quickly against them in Barbados and Granada. I'm not sure how quick I was bowling and sometimes the speed gun doesn't always show how fast you are.'

But there were other moments when Bond proved he belonged, one of them coming when the Australian captain, Steve Waugh, strode to the crease with the score at an imposing 3/266. Bond, who at that stage had played just twenty-one first-class matches, figured he didn't have a lot to lose, so he bent the back and welcomed the skipper with a couple of short ones.

'Here I was bowling to a legend, someone I had been watching and admiring since I was a kid. But I bowled a couple where he was just a little uncomfortable on the back foot. I was never someone who would say anything to the batsman, maybe just a bit of a stare or something, but after I hit his hand Steve Waugh had a go at me, which really took me aback. It wasn't something I had experienced from a batsman before, and I never did again,' recalls Bond.

Shane Bond

HITTING BATSMEN

'I never set out to strike a batsman and didn't find it very pleasant when that happened. Early on in my career I knocked a bloke out and he didn't come back. There were broken fingers, arms, teeth, all the way through school. None of it was real pleasant. But instinct tells you when they don't like it short, and you try and push different buttons when you have that extra pace. You hit them on the thigh or backside, you see them grimace and you go, "That's good!" I don't like to see them hit on the head and hurt or something. I am the first one to run across. But the times when they are jumping around, you walk back to your mark with a smile. No one truly enjoys facing fast bowling.'

'It was actually quite funny. Clearly he was just trying to throw me off my stride. I remember thinking I was playing against all these great players and that it couldn't get any tougher. I figured as long as I could complete then, I would be okay at that level. That confrontational stuff I quite enjoy watching, but it just wasn't my personality.'

A few balls after Bond struck Waugh, the Australian skipper shouldered arms to an inswinger just outside off-stump. It prompted a massive LBW appeal that received an affirmative upwards finger, providing Bond with his first Test scalp and beginning a whirlwind career that burnt brightly, yet all too shortly.

Some of his finest work came in the shorter forms of the game, with Bond truly believing he belonged after a rip-snorting yorker knocked

Shane Bond

Shane Bond

back Gilchrist's leg stump in a VB series game in 2002. 'That one ball changed my whole thinking. Before that I was still intimidated, but after that I started to believe that I was up to that standard. I went from worrying about bowling a half-volley to backing myself to be the best fast bowler in the world.'

Bond is too modest to suggest he ever claimed that tag, but his One Day strike rate of 29.22 (with 147 wickets at just 20.88) remains the testing material for any bowler. In fact in whatever length of game Bond played, he took wickets and he took them often – consider his Test strike rate, a remarkable 38.76.

He had grown up idolising New Zealand's greatest fast bowler in Richard Hadlee, later to become Sir Richard, such were his cricketing deeds. Not that Bond was anything more than a smallish lad through school, one who could bowl quickish without ever providing his schoolmates with nightmares. Like many before and after him, Bond tried to copy the actions of the leading quicks of the time. For a while his run-up was long, with a desire to bowl super quick inswinging yorkers like Waqar Younis.

A day later he had become a pale imitation of South Africa's 'White Lightning', Allan Donald, attempting to bowl outswing at a blistering pace, before moving closer to home by impersonating fellow Kiwi

Shane Bond

Bond's
BEST BATSMEN

SHANE WATSON AND GRAEME SMITH

'They were both able to hook or pull me and were in position so quickly.'

AB DE VILLIERS

'Another who was hard to bowl to because he was so quick on the short ball.'

SACHIN TENDULKAR

'Because he was short, he was hard for me to find the right length to bowl to.'

RAHUL DRAVID

'Just didn't seem to make any mistakes back in the early and mid-2000s. Dravid was incredibly tough.'

BRIAN LARA AND RICKY PONTING

'Great batsmen, who I actually got out a few times. In Lara's case it was normally because he was out of form when we played them. It was funny in international cricket because there were certain great players you felt like you were all over. Others you never thought you would get out.'

Shane Bond

Bond's
BEST BOWLERS

DALE STEYN, WASIM AKRAM AND GLENN MCGRATH

'Has to compare with the greatest of any era, as good as just about anyone to play. If I was picking three bowlers to open my dream attack they would be Dale Steyn, Wasim Akram, who every second batsmen I speak to says is the greatest ever, and I would have to put Glenn McGrath in there because he was just unbelievable for consistency of performance.'

BRETT LEE

'I loved watching Brett Lee bowl. He had extreme fitness and bio-mechanically was very sound, working in straight lines.'

ANDREW FLINTHOFF

'Bowled a very heavy ball.'

SIR RICHARD HADLEE

'If you were looking for the perfect action, I couldn't go past Sir Richard Hadlee, who finished his career before me. He bowled so close to the stumps, moved the ball around, was accurate and could produce a really good short ball. He had unique physical characteristics, such as his feet being splayed out, which allowed him to do things with the ball.'

Shane Bond

Danny Morrison. By the time he was sixteen, Bond got the opportunity to check out his action courtesy of video. He didn't like what he saw. 'When I first saw my action I was shocked. I had given up all those other guys and settled on Sir Richard Hadlee, and in my mind I bowled just like him. But what I saw was a mess.' Bond laughs.

'Right from when I was a kid I had wanted to bowl fast, but my action was "frog in a blender" stuff. The only element of Sir Richard that my action included was my arm going back over my head. Then I realised who I looked like. Me. And sadly it was a poor technique which, when coupled with a lack of fitness, meant seven stress fractures in my back between ages seventeen and twenty-nine. I was lazy, and I didn't have the heart to run in and bowl consistently quick.'

Like many teenage boys he was a late developer, not really growing until his mid-teens. That's when it all came together and he began to

Shane Bond

Justin Langer
ON BOND

'Shane Bond bowled a very heavy ball. He was very strong and hit the bat harder than most bowlers of that era. And he was a handful for left-handers because his natural delivery took the ball away from us. Whenever you played him you knew you were in for a fight because he was such a good competitor. We certainly treated him with respect every time he was on the field but it was just a shame that his body wasn't able to hold up to the demands of international cricket.'

> 'It wasn't until I went away from cricket and came back at twenty-five that I became quick.'

get a name for being sharp, at least until his injury curse first struck at seventeen.

'I didn't really stand out in terms of pace until I was eighteen–nineteen, when my pace went up significantly. But when I started with Canterbury I was first change, and not overly quick. It wasn't until I went away from cricket and came back at twenty-five that I became quick,' explains Bond.

'I never thought I'd make it after a whole heap of fractures in my back. So I became a policeman. Once I got that security I decided I had missed cricket and would get myself fit. People started to say, "You are really getting the ball through." There were no speed guns back then, so when I first appeared on the international scene I spent half my time walking back, looking at the scoreboard to see how fast I had bowled. It took a while to break that habit, although it never completely goes away. It's an ego thing, to be fair.'

Shane Bond

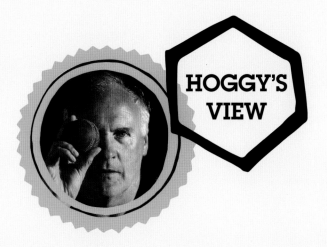

HOGGY'S VIEW

HE WAS THE QUICKEST BOWLER THE KIWIS HAVE EVER produced, although Sir Richard Hadlee was seriously quick when he wanted to be. Had I been able to coach Bond he would have been even better. To think that he can't remember the names of every batsman he hit: that is a disgrace for a quick. I have names dating back to fourth grade. An excuse for his lack of hatred towards batsmen may be that New Zealand is too far away from the mainland. It restricts their thinking. He just needed to brush shoulders with a few of the lunatics such as myself who played for Australia to realise how fast bowlers should act.

On a more serious note, cricket lovers worldwide were so frustrated Bond wasn't able to play more Test cricket. New Zealand's success rate when he played was a true indicator of his influence. In the eighteen Tests he played, they won ten and lost just two. Players like Bond can change your team's standing: a megastar who bowled the length and pace that really hurried batsmen, and like Dale Steyn he could move the ball away at genuine speed.

Shane Bond

JEFF THOMSON

'Thommo'

**Born 16 August 1950,
Greenacre, Sydney, New South Wales**

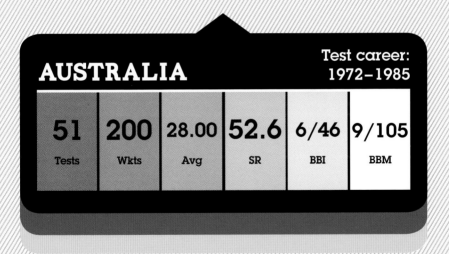

AUSTRALIA

Test career:
1972–1985

51	200	28.00	52.6	6/46	9/105
Tests	Wkts	Avg	SR	BBI	BBM

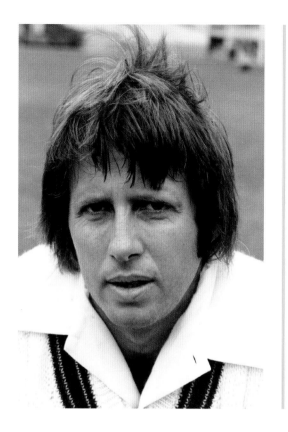

'Thomson is a natural phenomenon that the resilient background of Australian cricket throws up from time to time. He is, however, the happy warrior, the person every real fast bowler should be.'

WHILE HIS WORDS MAY HAVE LACKED THE SUBTLETY of a poet laureate, it's doubtful anyone better instilled fear into an opposition than Jeff Thomson on the eve of the 1974/75 Ashes series in Australia. Of course, that fierceness was far removed from the real personality of Thomson, a genial soul who is much-loved in the cricketing world. But back in November 1974, he was a young bloke trying to make the most of his second crack at Test cricket, and anything or anyone that stood in his way had better look out.

What Thomson came to represent in the mid-1970s is best encapsulated by a meeting between 41-year-old Colin Cowdrey, later to be awarded a CBE, knighthood and peerage (Baron Cowdrey of Tonbridge), and 24-year-old Thomson in the second Test of the 1974/75 Ashes series at the WACA in Perth. Cowdrey had been preparing for a white Christmas in his native Kent when the call came

Jeff Thomson

through that his courage and technique were required to quell an uprising in the colonies. That he hadn't played Test cricket for near-on four years mattered little to the desperate English selectors. They had seen Cowdrey stand up to the best that Ray Lindwall, Keith Miller, Neil Adcock, Peter Heine, Sir Wes Hall and Charlie Griffith had thrown at him, in a career that had begun twenty years earlier at the Gabba.

Michael Colin Cowdrey was eleven days shy of his forty-second birthday when his portly figure strode to the wicket, his very name baring the initials of the Marylebone Cricket Club. There to greet him was Jeffrey Robert 'call me Thommo' Thomson, an athletic, surfie-looking type who liked to hunt pigs – someone who seemed to typify the uncouth inbreds of the colonies. While Cowdrey had studied geography as a resident in Brasenose College at Oxford University, Thomson's academic achievements at Punchbowl Boys High School were considerably more modest, his schooling best described as 'sporadic'.

The pair had never met, although when first told that Cowdrey was on a mercy flight to Australia, Thomson said, 'He'll cop it too.'

On arrival at the crease, the ever-polite Cowdrey quickly offered his hand, accompanied by the words, 'Good morning, Mr Thomson, my name is Cowdrey.' A bemused Thomson accepted the handshake before returning to his fourteen-pace mark, muttering to himself about this pathetic peace offering from a man who was clearly petrified. 'Good luck, fatso, if you think that's going to do you any good,' is the reply Thomson recollects these days, but he readily admits he underestimated a man who was always prepared to get behind the dangerous projectiles. Cowdrey scored 22 and 41, actually putting his hand up to open the second innings. He went on to play all four remaining Tests, and while 41 remained his top score, Cowdrey won much respect for his courage. As for Thomson, the legend had been born after 33 wickets in just four and a half Tests, before he injured his shoulder ligaments playing tennis on the rest day of the fifth Test.

Jeff Thomson

To say Thomson was a surprise is a serious understatement, although the English captain, the late Mike Denness, had an inkling things could become dire prior to the first Test, when in the tour game with Queensland he was struck on the collarbone by a rearing Thomson delivery. Desperate to show no sign of pain, the elegant right-hander batted on. Only after his dismissal did he notice that a gold St Christopher pendant had become embedded in his chest by the force of the thunderbolt. At the time Denness kept this to himself, concerned such knowledge would do little to ease the anxieties of his teammates.

To the touring Englishmen, Thomson seemed to get faster as the series progressed, and reports being tabled back to the UK painted him as the devil incarnate, when in fact most English players enjoyed his company once they had got to know him.

> 'I was half-pissed when they timed me at 160km/h in one of those bowling speed contests.'

Frank Tyson, who alongside Sir Wes Hall was universally regarded as the fastest person to ever visit Australian shores, sums Thomson up in typically eloquent fashion: 'Thomson is a natural phenomenon that the resilient background of Australian cricket throws up from time to time. He is, however, the happy warrior, the person every real fast bowler should be.'

'I was half-pissed when they timed me at 160km/h in one of those bowling speed contests,' Thomson recalls. 'I was banned from playing and sitting in the box, having a drink, when Kerry Packer came in and said, "Thommo, what are you fucking doing here?" I said, "What else can I do? I've got a bung shoulder." He said "No, no, no, the fast-bowling thing is on." I told him I wasn't allowed to bowl, and he said, "Get fucked. I run this joint, so get your arse down there and you better bloody win." So I borrowed some gear from someone my

Jeff Thomson

Thomson's
BEST BOWLERS

MITCH JOHNSON

'It was good to see him get a bit of mongrel back. For a while there he was going through the motions when his action was terrible, his arm was too low. I don't know why it took until the end of his career for someone to do something about it.'

MICHAEL HOLDING

'Just so smooth. I reckon being such a good bloke hindered Michael Holding a bit. If he had the attitude of Andy Roberts or Colin Croft, then he would have got twice as many wickets.'

MALCOLM MARSHALL

'The best out of all of us in my time.'

JOEL GARNER

'The big bloke was always a handful, plus he could field well anywhere. And he was just a good bloke.'

size after six cans and watched these pricks bowling bouncers. I knew quickly you had to pitch it up. It was the easiest ten grand I ever made,' he adds, laughing.

Whether Thomson was faster than bowlers such as Tyson and Hall can never be accurately determined, but what made Thomson different was his innate ability to make balls explode off a good length. Others came after him such as West Indian Patrick Patterson – searingly fast but gun-barrel straight, with a traditional action where the ball was on display

Jeff Thomson

Jeff Thomson

prior to delivery. At times Patterson may have even rivalled Thomson for sheer pace, but that's where the similarities end.

In the early days Thomson didn't care much about the nuances of swing. He could move the ball, even if it took him a couple of seasons at the top level before he learnt where to place the shining side to create an outswinger. 'Just trot up and go *wang*' was Thomson's mantra, and he did so for a decade at extreme pace. But what he also did (particularly before the collision with Alan 'Fitter'n'Turner' that left him with a dislocated collarbone) was make the ball fizz off a length. And at his pace that made him unplayable when he hit the right spot.

The view is that Thomson's lift came from an action that has never been successfully duplicated, but one that might be the purest and most effective of all. As side-on as he could possibly be, his left arm pointing to the heavens and his left leg raised like that of a javelin thrower, Thomson looked as if he belonged in the Olympics, and it is no surprise when you learn he was school athletics champion plus a school representative for soccer, a game he loved.

> 'Just trot up and go *wang*' was Thomson's mantra, and he did so for a decade at extreme pace.

'I could bowl quick without even training,' says Thomson. 'I had flexibility and was reasonably strong without working on it. I'm probably more flexible now than most of them. You need to be an athlete to do it. Some blokes can't even touch their toes. Brett Lee is an athlete and that's why he has played until forty.'

Thomson's early progression through the ranks was quick, only stifled by his lackadaisical approach to training – or even club games – whenever the lure of surfing, fishing or chasing girls took hold. The strong New South Wales side meant that state selection eluded him until he was finally selected to play against Queensland in 1972/73. Seven Shield

Jeff Thomson

Thomson's
BEST BATSMEN

SIR VIV RICHARDS

'Played me best when I was at my fastest. But before I got my shoulder done everyone was on the hustle, Barry Richards and whoever. Ring them and ask if you doubt me.'

THE CHAPPELL BROTHERS [GREG AND IAN]

'Blokes who had a bit more time than others, who went back rather than going forward. The Chappells had the best techniques of all of them. Get on the back foot and it gives you all sorts of options. You can still go forward and drive if you take a big enough step forward. It makes me laugh to see these blokes keep getting on the front foot these days. I would have loved to see them doing that against me.'

games later, he was chosen to play Pakistan at the MCG alongside Dennis Lillee and Max Walker. But with match figures of 0/110 and a broken left foot, his summer was over, and maybe his Test career. So he got himself right over winter and started bowling as quickly as he had in his life, but was still ignored by the New South Wales state selectors right up until the final match against Queensland in Sydney.

If the visitors won it would be their first ever Shield, as their captain Greg Chappell recalls: 'I wish they had stuck to their initial policy and not picked Thommo at all, because he took 7/85 and won the game. That spell was the quickest I faced in my career, no doubt. Michael Holding was very slippery in a game in Launceston in fading light, but Thommo was the fastest. Since then maybe Shaun Tait got close in a couple of spells, but Thommo did it for a long period.'

Jeff Thomson

Chappell decided then and there that he didn't want to experience Thomson the opponent again and quickly got things in motion so he could join Queensland. And that was where wicketkeeper John Maclean first kept to him.

'In that last game in Sydney when they brought him back, I reckon he bowled an eighteen-over spell where he kept getting quicker,' says Maclean. 'The first ball hit me in the shoulder – no helmets – when I hadn't even attempted to play a shot. I decided then it wasn't about making runs, but about survival.

'When he got quick it was ridiculous where I was standing. When he got his rhythm right he was frightening. Forget those speed guns, he was faster than 160km/h. I stood more than halfway to the boundary sometimes. Kerry O'Keeffe got an under edge that flew over my head and took one bounce before reaching the boundary. And bloody Thommo was asking Phil Carlson, "How are they coming off?" Phil said, "Pretty quickly, Thommo." He was blistering. Others, like Shaun Tait, might have been nearly as quick for an over and a half. But Thommo was such a good athlete that he could bowl 8–10 overs and actually get quicker. I honestly don't believe that anyone could ever have bowled quicker than Thommo. He was just a super athlete with that slinging action. You couldn't see the ball in his hand until the last second. Good luck after that.'

Thomson had copied the style from his father, Don, as did his four brothers Donny, Raymond, Gregory and Kevin. At the inaugural World Cup in 1975, Thomson caused three Sri Lankan batsmen to be carried from the ground with injuries. Australia lost that cup to the West Indies by 17 runs in a classic, prompting wild celebrations from the large West Indies supporter base living in London. As the players began to party on the podium, Thomson made it known to anyone within earshot that their time would come when they arrived in Australia for a six-Test series that summer. It was no idle threat, and the carnage inflicted

on the tourists in that Australian summer set the tone for West Indian fast-bowling gangs for the next two decades.

Thomson warmed up for that season with a spell against Western Australia in Perth that is still spoken of. Opening batsman Bruce 'Stumpy' Laird, who was renowned for both technique and courage, well recalls it: 'We hadn't lost a game for a fair while at that stage, but we lost that one after he took 11 wickets. He hit me on the shoulder, and I actually didn't see the ball, which was the only time in my career when I didn't pick up a delivery. It was sheer speed, and we didn't have helmets. I reckon around 1975/76 he was at his peak, before he hurt his shoulder. He was still very quick after that injury, but beforehand he had a higher arm action and got more bounce. Afterwards his arm was just a bit lower, meaning he didn't explode off a good length. If he got it all together he could get the ball to climb, whereas with others you could judge their length and play accordingly.

'I played the West Indies a fair bit, and Michael Holding was the quickest. Andy Roberts was probably the best of them because he did a bit more with it and swung it away. But Andy was probably around 145km/h

Jeff Thomson

whereas Thommo and Holding were definitely 150km/h-plus bowlers. What you found in the 1970s was bowlers like Thommo never tried to insult you. He wasn't that sort of bloke, in fact he never said a word. These days they sledge ten times as much, and it's getting out of control.' Thomson agrees: 'I don't remember abusing batsmen much. I would rather shut up and keep them guessing so they didn't know what they were going to cop.

'They say I was pretty quick in the West Indies at Barbados but I don't think I was ever as quick after I did my shoulder. I was never the same. I'd just been getting quicker all the time, and it was getting easier by age twenty-six until I got run into by a tortoise [Australian batsman Alan Turner]. I was a bit unlucky but I wasn't bitter at the time. I remember hearing the doctor in the dressing-room say that I wouldn't play again. It was the best thing I could have heard because it drove me to prove them wrong. All I wanted to do was get my shoulder pulled back into place so I could go back out to finish them off.'

> 'What you found in the 1970s was bowlers like Thommo never tried to insult you. He wasn't that sort of bloke.'

Thomson may have been a different bowler after that injury in the summer of 1976/77, but the spectators at Kensington Oval in Bridgetown, Barbados, fourteen months later, might beg to differ. His 6/77 from 13 overs, including the scalps of Gordon Greenidge, Sir Viv Richards and Alvin Kallicharran, remains one of those withering spells that the Barbadians have passed on through time. 'Ooh man, that Jeffrey Robert Thomson. He got pace like fire,' is how the locals remember Thommo. As their captain Clive Lloyd once explained, the best way to handle Thomson was to get to the other end.

Jeff Thomson

143

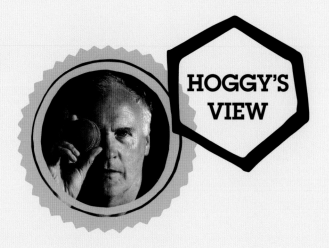

HOGGY'S VIEW

THE TWO FASTEST BALLS I ever received were courtesy of Jeffrey Robert Thomson in 1977/78, after he had done his shoulder. I'm one of those rare cricketers who can actually admit they were petrified when facing really quick bowling, but normally the fear took hold of me as they started to run in. In Thommo's case I started shaking when I arrived at the crease and could hardly see wicketkeeper John Maclean because he was standing so far back. I had to yell so Maclean could hear me when I asked why he was standing so far away. He smiled and said, 'You'll find out, mate.'

The first ball I honestly didn't see. Apparently it just shaved my off-stump. I had never met Thommo before then – if I had, I would have offered him money to slow down. Fortunately the second one (which remains a blur) bowled me and I could get the hell out of there. Thommo was just *that* quick – and I faced Andy Roberts, Michael Holding, Joel Garner, Colin Croft, Malcolm Marshall and Wayne Daniel. He was quicker, don't worry.

Thommo had the perfect action for delivering a missile at extreme pace, but I'm sure you could only do it if you had the perfect athletic body like a Keith Miller, Brett Lee or Mitchell Johnson. He was similar to Wasim Akram in that his run-up gave you no real

Jeff Thomson

England's Tony Greig narrowly avoids being hit in the face by a Jeff Thomson ball.
Old Trafford, Manchester, 1977.

suggestion of what was to come, but Akram at least sprinted for his ten paces. Thommo was like facing a moving bowling machine set on 160km/h. Another part of the problem was you lost sight of the ball in his delivery stride. As a person he is very easy-going. There was nothing nasty about him on the field, other than the fact he bowled so quickly.

In Thommo's case I started shaking when I arrived at the crease and could hardly see wicketkeeper John Maclean because he was standing so far back.

Jeff Thomson

145

FRANK TYSON

'Typhoon'

**Born 6 June 1930,
Farnworth, Lancashire**

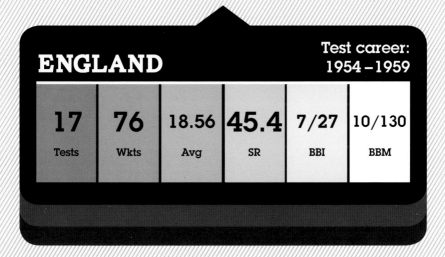

ENGLAND				Test career: 1954 –1959	
17	76	18.56	**45.4**	7/27	10/130
Tests	Wkts	Avg	SR	BBI	BBM

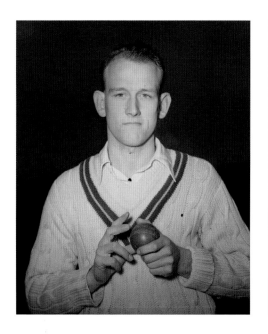

At his prime in 1954 he was the fastest bowler in the world, and when they're that quick they are difficult.

AS HIS NICKNAME OF 'TYPHOON' IMPLIES, FRANK

Holmes Tyson was a violent storm that struck with force before departing oh so swiftly, and yet is still spoken of with awe sixty years later.

Just as Fred 'the Demon' Spofforth and Harold Larwood had before him, Tyson instilled rare fear into the hearts and minds of the game's finest batting practitioners. Even the most artistic of batsmen – in Tyson's time a Neil Harvey or Keith Miller – who seemed to see the ball that little bit earlier would occasionally be late on their shot when facing the Typhoon. If evidence was needed, no fewer than 33 of Tyson's 76 Test wickets were bowled, a remarkable percentage that was no doubt the result of beating players through sheer pace.

Australia's brave and technically correct opener Colin McDonald has never forgotten his first sighting of the Typhoon: 'We were playing a tour match against Frank Tyson's county of Northamptonshire on the Ashes tour of 1953. We had been warned on arriving in England that there was this fellow called Tyson who was pretty quick, so it was in the back of our minds, but not something we were losing any sleep over. I was about to play the first delivery when it caught the edge of my bat and flew to the boundary. The next ball struck me on the leg. And it hurt: one because I was out, and another because of the pace it struck me at.

'A couple of balls later he bowled Graeme Hole before Graeme could get his bat down. The stumps went everywhere and we knew then that he was going to be a handful in years to come, even if he didn't do much else in that game.'

QUICKEST SPELL

'Probably early on when I first joined Northants after a year playing for Knypersley. I was fresh from university and raring to go. After that I would have to say Sydney in 1954/55. From that tour on I had a bad run with injury, mainly due to an ankle problem, and I never really bowled with the same speed again. When I returned to Australia in 1959 I was about the same pace as our first-change bowler, Trevor Bailey. My peak years should have been between 1956 and 1960 but I missed a lot of cricket in that time.

But I remain very proud of both my strike rate and Test average. Those great English players when Test cricket was in its infancy, bowlers such as Sydney Barnes and George Lohmann, had similar strike rates. That time they talk about when I hit the sightscreen might have happened more than once. I can remember bowling a bouncer to South Africa's Roy McLean at Old Trafford in 1955 when that definitely occurred. Our wicketkeeper Godfrey Evans didn't get near it.'

Frank Tyson

Tyson's
BEST BATSMEN

NEIL HARVEY

'The best I bowled to. He was known as a great player of spin but he played fast bowling equally as well. If we didn't get Harvey out early, by the end of the day he would be 150.'

LEN HUTTON

'Wasn't as destructive as Harvey but a great defensive player.'

ARTHUR MORRIS

'A wonderful defensive player.'

SIR DON BRADMAN

'Of course we are talking about everyone other than Don Bradman because he belongs on his own.'

COLIN COWDREY

'Very natural with the bat. You could close your eyes and just listen to the exquisite sound of the ball hitting bat. So sweet.'

DENIS COMPTON

'An entertainer. Completely irrepressible. He would improvise.'

SIR GARRY SOBERS

'I bowled to him in 1956 when he was batting down the order. He and Bradman were the greatest cricketers ever.'

GRAHAM YALLOP

'Of the Test players I coached at schoolboy level, he was the best because of his rare timing. He was a classical batsman. I never found out why he didn't play more for Australia.'

Frank Tyson

Welcome to a force of mass destruction, devastatingly fast on his day, and even now evoking a combination of fear and respect in those who faced him at the peak of his powers in the Australian summer of 1954/55.

Neil Harvey, regarded by many as his country's finest left-handed batsman, says he can't imagine anyone bowling faster than Tyson did on the 1954/55 tour of Australia.

'At his prime in 1954 he was the fastest bowler in the world, and when they're that quick they are difficult. At that period he was the bowler who was going to get the good players out. In the third Test in Melbourne the pitch was so bad that you could disregard those performances due to the cracks in the wicket, but in Sydney he was serious, very serious,' says Harvey.

'He bowled a lot of bouncers and didn't give you too many half-volleys. Bowlers of Tyson's pace – Wes Hall, Jeff Thomson, those type of players – there wouldn't be much between their paces at all. Once you start bowling at that speed, you really can't go much quicker than anyone else. Tyson was as quick as I ever faced, along with Wes Hall. I wouldn't like to separate them. The thing with Frank is he didn't last that long. He came back but wasn't as dangerous.'

Tyson was born in Farnworth, Lancashire, on 6 June 1930 and was raised in a household where cricket wasn't the addiction it was for so many of the men he would later play with and against. He was encouraged to read and found a whole new world in the works of George Bernard Shaw and Geoffrey Chaucer, and the poet William Wordsworth, a man he would sometimes quote out in the middle. It distances him from other men of express speed, such as the coalminer's son Harold Larwood or

> 'Once you start bowling at that speed, you really can't go much quicker than anyone else.'

Frank Tyson

151

Frank Tyson (right) Brian Statham (left) leading the England cricket team off the pitch after a victory against Australia. SCG, Sydney, 1954.

Australia's Jeff Thomson, whose grammar was far more perfunctory (for Thommo, the question was why you would use all those big words when a couple of four-lettered ones could do the job). Tyson's education meant he didn't always react the way headstrong quicks were expected to.

When he toured Australia in 1954/55 he was physically ready to impact the series, helped by the fact he increased his weight by 10 kilograms within six weeks of leaving England, which had just ended food rationing. Much was made of the pain he was going to inflict on the Australians, claims that appeared very tepid after he went for 1/160 off 29 eight-ball overs in Australia's first innings of 8/601. But the scoreline in Brisbane, with England losing by an innings and 154 runs, camouflaged the vital fact that Tyson had struck Arthur Morris and Neil Harvey on several occasions.

Frank Tyson

> 'The ball skidded through and hit me a sickening blow on the back of my head.'

In the second Test in Sydney a Ray Lindwall short ball hit Tyson. His memory of the blow is vivid: 'It was fast and short, prompting me to turn. The ball skidded through and hit me a sickening blow on the back of my head. I hit the ground and started to slip in and out of consciousness. It didn't help much when I heard my batting partner, Bill Edrich, telling Lindy [Lindwall] that he had killed me. I was angry, very angry, and knew that I would be repaying Lindwall and his teammates. They took me to hospital for X-rays because I had this huge bump on my head. Then they cleared me and I returned before being bowled by Lindwall.'

When Australia batted they prepared for a bumper barrage, but Tyson the scholar was too smart, keeping the ball pitched up when steaming in from the Randwick end, wind at his back and as fast as young Australian all-rounder Richie Benaud had ever seen. With his opening partner, Brian Statham, typically keeping things tight from the other end, Tyson claimed 6/85 and match figures of 10/130 to bowl England to victory. Four of six victims in Jim Burke, Graeme Hole, Ron Archer and Lindwall were bowled.

It was a victory for clear thinking, even if Tyson admits he was never the bowler his English teammate Fred Trueman was: 'Fred always said to me that I might have been faster but he was the better bowler, and he was right because he *was* a far better bowler than me. Exercising your intelligence is normally far more effective than brute strength.'

Tyson's bowling on that tour was pivotal in England's 3/1 triumph. He took 28 wickets at 20.82 (some average after his first Test hammering) and was later named one of Wisden's five cricketers of the year alongside Colin Cowdrey, Doug Insole, Jackie McGlew and

Frank Tyson

Hugh Tayfield. It also saw Sir Donald Bradman nominate Tyson as the fastest bowler he had seen, a view he later revisited when adding Jeff Thomson to the same bracket.

On that Australian tour it appeared the cricketing world was Tyson's oyster, making it all the more surprising that he played just eleven more Tests over four summers. There were still times when the Typhoon blew its hardest, such as at Trent Bridge in 1955 against the South Africans where he claimed 2/38 and 6/40, or two years later at St George's Park, where he ran through the same opponents with 2/51 and 6/28.

> There were still times when the Typhoon blew its hardest.

But then he was gone, his 76 Test wickets coming at an average of just 18.56 in seventeen matches. Tyson believes he was a victim of his environment and action. 'I bowled for a county in Northampton that had three good spinners, so the wickets were flat and hardly conducive to my style of bowling. At Northants I was basically the only fast bowler, because we had George Tribe, Mickey Allen and Jack Manning, who were spinners. I would bowl a few overs, then those boys would come on. I only ever took 100 wickets in a season once, in 1957,' recalls Tyson. 'The wickets were flat and hard work, plus I had an unusual action that put pressure on me. And then there was a constant ankle injury because I couldn't find the right footwear. I would have been fine if I were playing today.'

On that tour Tyson loved Australia, and Australians, and six years later he migrated to Melbourne. There he became a history and French teacher at Carey Baptist Grammar, numbering among his students a future Australian Test captain named Graham Yallop.

Australian humour appealed to Tyson, as on the occasion when he dined at The Lodge prior to a tour match against the Prime Minister's XI. His

Tyson's
BEST BOWLERS

RAY LINDWALL

'He hit me on the back of the head in Sydney in 1954/55. I had to retire, and it did fire me up. But I admired him tremendously – he was a master of his craft. Gubby Allen wanted me to bowl at the leg stump and hit the off, as that's what Lindwall could do.'

ANDY ROBERTS

'Impressed me as a very astute bowler, one who could detect a batsman's weakness very quickly, then exploit it.'

FRED SPOFFORTH

'My dream opening attack. I would travel back in time to see him.'

WASIM AKRAM

'A great bowler because of his pace, his movement, his control.'

JEFF THOMSON

'Obviously you would come up with Thommo because of the speed at which he bowled; on the other hand, you could have someone like Keith Miller who would win matches for you because he knew how to get batsmen out.'

FRED TRUEMAN

'He would be very high on the list, not because of his speed but because of what he did with the ball.'

MIKE PROCTER

'Could be a handful because he was just so strong. Plus he could swing it at pace and bowl a good short ball.'

Frank Tyson

reputation had preceded him, and when the former Australian captain Lindsay Hassett spoke, he mentioned the English fast bowler named the Typhoon. On cue the skies responded with a tremendous roar of thunder. Never one to miss such an opportunity, Hassett responded, 'Ah, there's the bugger now, starting his run-up.'

Tyson's first-class debut had come three years earlier against the touring Indians, who were said to be concerned when the wicketkeeper moved halfway back to the sightscreen to receive Tyson. Legend has it he once hit the Old Trafford sightscreen on the full after the ball had pitched and taken off. Jeff Thomson is said to have done the same, and a wild-eyed West Indian, Roy Gilchrist, whose temperament never allowed his freight-train pace to be harnessed.

Tyson still believes he was first selected at Test level after he hospitalised Bill Edrich at Lords; the popular opener was beaten for speed on the hook and ended up with a fractured cheekbone. With pain can come gain, and Tyson knew he could create havoc if used in short spells: 'You can't have a tearaway quick plugging away all day. He must be saved for sharp bursts, and then brought back refreshed for second and third spells, just like Michael Clarke did with Mitchell Johnson against England and South Africa.'

Frank Tyson bowls to Roy Marshall in his last match for Northampton. Dean Park, Bournemouth, 1960.

Frank Tyson

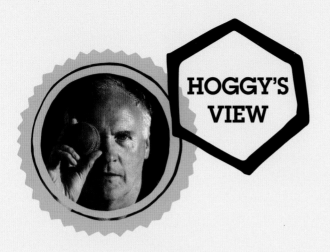

HOGGY'S VIEW

BEFORE WE MET I DIDN'T LIKE HIM BECAUSE HE HAD

two things I lacked: firstly, a really catchy nickname in 'Typhoon' Tyson that implied fearsome speed. Secondly, an ability to speak fluent French (and English for that matter), which he taught at Carey Grammar when he immigrated to Australia as a ten-pound Pom. Okay, I wasn't the scholar that Frank was, but why couldn't some journalist or teammate have christened me 'Hurricane' Hogg? Has a nice ring to it …

Sorry, back to Frank. He was always very encouraging to me, and it gives any young quick confidence when one of the Kings of Speed says something positive. If pushed I suspect he may have been at least the equal quickest of anyone to ever bowl, alongside Jeff Thomson. I didn't see him at his peak in 1954/55, but I've spoken to enough batsmen who faced him and have no doubt he worked up around the 160km/h range. A lot of his pace seemed to come from brute strength: one of those strongly built quicks like Sir Wes Hall and Sylvester Clarke.

From the footage I have seen it looks like he had a classical side-on action: high left arm and plenty of activity when he reached delivery stride. When you think of the two fastest bowlers of the first sixty years of the 20th century, they were two Englishmen, Harold Larwood and Frank Tyson. But really there has not been an Englishman as quick since.

Frank Tyson

157

LEN PASCOE

'Slippery'

Born 13 February 1950,
Bridgetown North, Western Australia

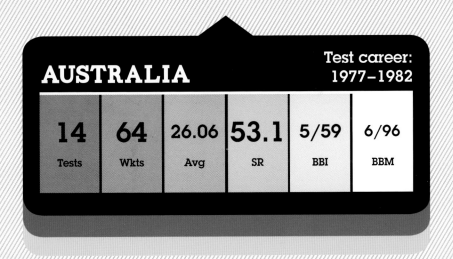

AUSTRALIA				Test career: 1977–1982	
14	64	26.06	53.1	5/59	6/96
Tests	Wkts	Avg	SR	BBI	BBM

Just the type you feared in the playground as a youngster, when reputations were formed on who showed the most ticker when facing some mad-eyed quick.

LEN PASCOE WAS EVERYTHING A FAST BOWLER
should be: a broad-shouldered, 187cm figure of snorting, snarling aggression. Just the type you feared in the playground as a youngster, when reputations were formed on who showed the most ticker when facing some mad-eyed quick.

It was the same arena where young Leonard Stephen Pascoe (born Leonard Stephen Durtanovich) first realised the gift he had with a hard-cased ball. He became Lennie Pascoe, a young man who needed to be respected whenever he ran in to bowl.

When the Pascoe family moved to Sydney from Bridgetown in Western Australia, young Len had no real idea if he could play cricket. He and his brother had mucked around on their cousin's farm in the west with no inkling as to the nuances of the game, but he certainly heard plenty about it in Sydney.

Everywhere he went in the Bankstown area, the talk was about some kid called Grey, who was said to be a youthful incarnation of the feared English Bodyline bowler Harold Larwood. Pascoe hadn't witnessed the

Len Pascoe

Pascoe's
BEST BOWLERS

DENNIS LILLEE

'Really wrote the manual on how a fast bowler should bowl, but it took a broken back and eighteen months out of the game for Dennis to fully become the bowler we knew.'

MICHAEL HOLDING

'To face him off his long run-up was one of life's great pleasures, very scary, but wonderful all the same. I would be admiring the smoothness of his run-up and then remember I actually had to play a shot.'

ANDY ROBERTS

'Morose and brooding, cunning like a fox and finding a way when a wicket needed to be found.'

BOB WILLIS

'Awkward and bustling, like a turbo-charged Max Walker.'

GLENN MCGRATH

'His greatest gift was to evaluate, take what was necessary to achieve success and discard the rest.'

MITCHELL JOHNSON

'Today bowls the way that we did, with some serious attitude.'

RYAN HARRIS

'Has the closest attitude to me because he just keeps coming in even if he only has one leg. I really enjoy watching him bowl.'

Len Pascoe

demon Grey but he knew he was a seriously scary dude. So Grey was the boss, until one morning when a North Bankstown Primary School teacher named Miss Carroll instructed the boys to take their turns bowling a cork ball at her. Complete with high heels, she watched as the boys went through their paces, a collection of assorted actions, few if any looking like they were destined to one day walk on the hallowed grass of Lord's. Then Pascoe stepped up to deliver a ball that is still spoken of by wide-eyed witnesses. To Miss Carroll's credit she stood her ground as the Pascoe cannonball thudded into her ankle, before the pain saw her crumble to the ground. And so the legend of Lenny was born, the son of Macedonian immigrants had dethroned Grey, and the world better beware.

The word spread quickly as Pascoe started to run through opposition schools, some defeated before they faced a ball just because of the aura that surrounded any kid who could bowl fast. For Pascoe it was a badge of honour.

Len Pascoe

'I would be playing school cricket and would try to knock the stumps over to see how far back they went, and how far back the bails flew. Kids would say, "Gee, look how far back the stump went." I loved hearing it, and as you can imagine it was fodder for a fertile young mind,' says Pascoe, whose earliest cricket memories are listening to John Arlott and Brian Johnston describing the Ashes battle of the 1960s.

Pascoe was captivated by the headstrong Yorkshire fast bowler Fred Trueman, a man after his own heart. He saw Trueman as a rough diamond, a hard worker who was plying his trade on the cricket field. Pascoe was the son of a hard-working brick carter and was taught an ethic early that would remain with him, whether he was bowling the opening over at 11am or running in under a scorching sun for the last over before stumps.

> Pascoe was captivated by the headstrong Yorkshire fast bowler Fred Trueman, a man after his own heart.

Trueman never cared much about the pomp and ceremony of the game, more about giving the batsman a decent old hurry-up before knocking his middle peg out. He was a fast bowler with attitude, and for young Pascoe that was the goal. He would wander down to nearby Petersham Oval to escape his concrete surrounds, imagining he was Fred Trueman bowling on this grass oasis.

By his teenage years his physique, which future teammate Rodney Hogg described as the best in the game, was starting to take shape, and he got his nickname of 'Slippery'. Pascoe also met a local lad named Jeff Thomson, a partnership for Bankstown that would send tremors through Sydney Grade cricket for years to come.

'I had average ability but above-average attitude, and a good fast bowler needs to have attitude,' says Pascoe. 'It was the great

'We had the world's worst batting side so when it came our turn to bowl, we had to clean them up quickly.'

Englishman Harold Larwood who said to me, "I love the way you bowl, laddie, you've got the devil in you." That made me feel 10-foot tall, coming from him. I hadn't been coached a lot, and for me and Thommo it was just a matter of walking back and bowling as fast as you could.

'I realised I could cause damage very early in the piece, around sixteen when I was playing first grade for Bankstown with Thommo. We had the world's worst batting side so when it came our turn to bowl, we had to clean them up quickly. If they looked uncomfortable you knew they were on the skids. I have often been asked if I hate batsmen. The answer is no, but they stopped me from getting everything I wanted.'

Not that Pascoe always wanted to become a household cricketing name, as there was a time when his love for the game waned. He was spending hot afternoons waiting five or six hours to bat while his mates were cruising Sydney beaches, surfing and engaging in amorous pursuits.

'I had been picked to play the NSW Colts at age nineteen, but my mates kept coming back from these wild weekends telling me how much fun they were having, so I lost a bit of focus. The next thing I was twenty-five and my career was drifting away, until I had a conversation with a man named Warren Saunders who explained I was on my last chance. So I went for it because I knew that I was never going to be a doctor or a lawyer, and that cricket could give me the things I wanted in life.'

And so began an international career of considerable achievement, even if it was briefer than it could have been. Just fourteen Tests and twenty-nine One Day Internationals wasn't nearly enough for a bowler rated by Doug Walters as 'the fastest I've seen between 11am and 6pm'. Walters faced faster in individual spells, but never one who

Len Pascoe

Len Pascoe

Pascoe's
BEST BATSMEN

SIR VIV RICHARDS

'Just so powerful, with so much time to play his strokes. He intimidated you.'

IAN CHAPPELL

'He would goad you and then look to destroy you. He and Viv Richards didn't just destroy your bowling; they destroyed you as a person to see if you would crack under the pressure. I refused to do that and took them head-on.'

CLIVE LLOYD

'Majestic. He would hit a four off me and I would watch it and think, *gee, that was good*.'

GEOFF BOYCOTT

'Everyone found him annoying, but I didn't because I never thought he was going to tear me apart. It was usually the bloke at the other end who paid the price for Boycott's stubbornness.'

SUNIL GAVASKAR

'Like a surgeon, slicing and dicing, very wristy.'

GREG CHAPPELL

'Would sit on you for three overs, then you would try something silly and he would hit you for three fours. So incredibly patient.'

BARRY RICHARDS

'The bat in his hand was like an extra finger, just like Edward Scissorhands.'

Len Pascoe

maintained his pace throughout the day no matter what the workload, and he regrets that Pascoe didn't play more games alongside bowlers such as Lillee, Thomson and Hogg. As a person, Walters describes Pascoe as having 'a heap of good sides to him and only one bad side … when a cricket ball was in his hand'.

Walters would watch with amusement when Pascoe got steamed up, knowing that the short stuff would keep coming and that his captain would soon enough be pleading with him to pitch the ball up. When he did the results could be extreme, such as the 5/59 he took in the first innings of the 1980 Centenary Test at Lord's, four of them to LBWs. Greg Chappell, who was Pascoe's only captain at Test level, believes getting the best out of the quick was all about management.

'I recall during World Series Cricket he bowled four bouncers in a row to Viv Richards. My brother Ian had enough and yelled at him to start pitching the ball up. Lenny was pleading, "Please Ian, just one more, please, just one more." It was very funny to witness,' recalls Chappell.

> Walters describes Pascoe as having 'a heap of good sides to him and only one bad side … when a cricket ball was in his hand'.

'Lenny was at his best when he bowled just short of a length and is one of the best finishes I have seen in One Day cricket. It really came down to managing him properly. If left to his own devices he wasn't so effective, but managed properly he became a fabulous servant for Australian cricket. Not that we always got along. I can remember a Shield game between Queensland and New South Wales when he was no-balled and immediately told the umpire he was a word I can't say here.

'I quickly told Len his language was completely inappropriate, to which he replied, "Why don't you go and get stuffed too?" or words to that effect. Then he tried to kill me with every ball he bowled and when that didn't work, he was waiting for me the next morning outside the rooms wanting to go on with it. As luck would have it we had to sit next to each other on a trip to Perth for a Test match at the end of our game and it took me most of the trip to pacify Len.'

'Much of my career was wasted with poor technique,' says Pascoe now. 'If I had my time over I would be a stronger bowler today. I was at my quickest at age thirty-one, towards the end of my career. That was when I knocked out Sandeep Patel in Sydney, when I thought I had killed him. It was then that I decided to give the game away because I was becoming too aggressive and doing things on the field that I shouldn't have been doing. It was time to move on at thirty-two. A lot of us didn't survive World Series Cricket.'

PERFECT OVER

'Mine came playing 4th Grade as a fill-in when I coached Mossman. They were one short, I bowled one over to a fifteen-year-old kid and I did everything perfectly. The ball swung, cut and seamed. I didn't get him out, though.

There were times when I actually bowled quicker than Thommo, although I could never match his fastest ball because that was horrifyingly quick. He would have broken 160km/h easily. I could bowl in the mid-140s, early 150s, but I could maintain the aggression and strength for a long time.'

Len Pascoe

HOGGY'S VIEW

I'M DISAPPOINTED HE KNOCKED THAT TEACHER OVER when he was twelve. All I got at the same age was being chased with an umbrella by Mrs Bird at Hayes Park in Thornbury when I struck one of the Fairfield Methodists' batsmen. Lenny would have become a hero at school after that and never would have paid for a marble or lunch again.

I only played four Tests with him and the one that sticks out was against India at the SCG in 1981. They had this really stylish batsman, Sandeep Patil, who was beautiful to watch but suspect against a good short ball, even on the flat pitch. As a fast bowler you can sniff the fear and I quickly honed in on Patil, getting him a good one. I figured I'd drop him or take his wicket, or both, but Greg Chappell took me out and brought on Lenny, who bowled a peach and dropped Patil like a bag of spuds.

I can still recall the jealousy that swept through me. Everyone else rushed to Patil, while I remained at fine leg, covered in disappointment. People at the ground would have thought Lenny was quicker than me and that just couldn't be allowed. It was wrong that he got all the credit for dropping Patil because I'd softened him up. How quick was Lenny? Well they called him Slippery and it wasn't because he had a dubious nature. He could bowl as fast as the West Indians, aside from Michael Holding, often in the 145 to 150km/h range. He probably did bowl short too often but so did I so I'm not about to criticise him for that.

Len Pascoe

DEVON MALCOLM

Born 22 February 1963,
Kingston, Jamaica

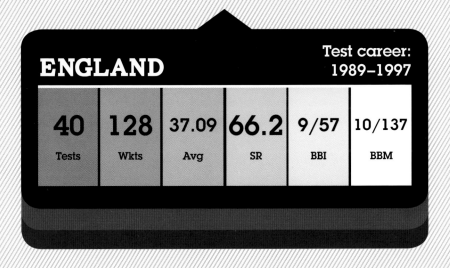

ENGLAND

Test career:
1989–1997

40	128	37.09	66.2	9/57	10/137
Tests	Wkts	Avg	SR	BBI	BBM

Broad-shouldered and bespectacled, Malcolm was known throughout his career as a kindly spoken man with a sunny nature, one you wouldn't think to associate with on-field carnage.

WHEN THE PLANETS ALIGNED, AND SUCH HAPPENINGS are rare in matters terrestrial, Devon Malcolm bowled with a fury that hurried all – and scared many – of the world's leading users of English willow.

Broad-shouldered and bespectacled, Malcolm was known throughout his career as a kindly spoken man with a sunny nature, one you wouldn't think to associate with on-field carnage. Yet when the conditions allowed and the mood took him, Malcolm bowled with a fiery intent that rivalled any of the great speed merchants before or since he made his debut against Australia at Trent Bridge, Nottingham, in the fifth Test of the 1989 Ashes series.

One need look no further than Malcolm's first two Tests to see the wide gaps that existed between best and worst. Brought into a hapless English team that had already failed to defend the Ashes, being 3/0 down after four Tests, Malcolm went wicketless on the opening day as Australian openers Geoff Marsh and Mark Taylor put on 310 by close of play. When that 329-run partnership was eventually

Devon Malcolm

LEARNING TO BOWL

'I wasn't coached too early, I just went and bowled as quickly as I could. At the start I didn't have boots or a bat, just a desire to compete harder than anyone else. Cricket now has all this video analysis and coaching. I learnt by looking and learning. My bowling was a combination of all my heroes': Garner, Holding, Lillee and Croft. I would jump wide like Croft. Then there was Jeff Thomson, the fastest I ever saw.

When I first went to England I didn't play cricket for two years. Where I lived, in Sheffield, everyone was playing football. I didn't start playing cricket until I was seventeen. They took me down to the nets and I bowled a few balls. The bloke said, "Who do you play for?" and I said, "No one." I started playing club and league cricket. I started to skittle people when I bowled straight. Then they told me I had something special and started to fine-tune me, but they also encouraged me to bowl fast. Michael Holding didn't believe in interfering much. He reckoned my body mechanisms allowed me to bowl the way I did. Apart from helping with a smooth run-up, he didn't believe in change for the textbook's sake.

My problem was having to run in hard on a hot day with big glasses bouncing around my head. I tried contact lenses but they never felt comfortable. Later on I had laser treatment and it made all the difference. I just wish I'd had it earlier in my career. My whole game changed, not just bowling but batting and fielding. The other thing I learnt was if I kept my wrist behind the ball then I could still bowl at good pace and move it. I could swing it late and consistently. I don't kid myself that I was one of the greats but I like to think that opposition teams respected me for trying as hard as I could on any type of pitch.'

Devon Malcolm

Malcolm's
BEST BATSMEN

BRIAN LARA

'Once he got to 10–20 you just knew he was going to get 80, and once he got there you were expecting 120. He could play every shot but he also had the ability to make very big scores. An unbelievable player.'

SIR VIV RICHARDS

'He was the most aggressive, and I bowled to him when he was past his peak. It's rare for a batsman to intimidate bowlers, but Viv did. He intimidated me and I was meant to be intimidating him. He just told me very calmly what he was going to do and then did it. He said, "Dev, it's SHOWTIME", after my first delivery, which was a dot ball. He then took 19 off the next five.'

STEVE WAUGH

'A gutsy player. People he said he didn't like the short stuff, but it was a waste of time bowling it to him. If I had his concentration then I would have been a much better bowler. I really admired him as a batsman.'

DAVID GOWER

'One of my heroes because he was so elegant. A magnificent player.'

Devon Malcolm

broken, Malcolm continued his fruitless toil until David Gower caught Steve Waugh for an eight-ball duck to give him his sole scalp in innings figures of 1/166 from 44 overs.

The Australians were familiar with Devon Eugene Malcolm, having encountered him in a tour game against Derbyshire. One Ian Healy, Australian wicketkeeper/batsman, well recalls: 'We were first exposed to him in 1989 when he played Derby just prior to the first Test and he rocked us there. I remember him bowling a head-high full toss at AB [captain Allan Border] when I was batting and thinking, *what is going to happen here?*

'Then in 1993 he played the last Test at The Oval, which Michael Slater still talks about as being the fastest he faced. Devon was awkward. Part of it was he didn't really look at you when you were facing. When you were the non-striker he almost seemed to be looking at you. Then all of

a sudden, *woosh*. You would think the ball wasn't going to come at you, and quite often it didn't, but every now and then it did. Very quickly. He was capable of real pace.

'I wouldn't put him ahead of Malcolm Marshall, Curtly Ambrose or Courtney Walsh, but it wouldn't surprise me if he was actually faster than any of them on his day. Or even just in one over, one spell or one ball. Sometimes it just clicked. He was certainly a talking point in our dressing-rooms, as he would have been in the English rooms. That was

Devon Malcolm

Devon Malcolm

the enigma of Dev. He could bowl not-so-fast or hit you in the head. We would be sitting there talking about how fast he could bowl, hoping it wouldn't click. And the English would be talking about the same thing, but praying he did click.'

And click he did in his second Test six months later when England toured the West Indies, a homecoming for the 27-year-old twelve years after he had joined his father in England. To be back in Jamaica was special for Malcolm, even if his team was given no chance against a side that had ruled the world for the previous fifteen years. He was suddenly back in the city where he was born, surrounded by friends and family, some of whom he didn't know existed.

'It was just a special feeling,' Malcolm explains. 'There were all these relatives I had never heard of, plus schoolmates I hadn't seen for years and even schoolteachers. It is such a big thing over there. They didn't know if I could bowl or not but they wanted to be there anyway. The thing that hits you most is how loud the crowd is, but once they realised I could bowl quickly, and the moment I got Viv Richards out [LBW], you could have heard a pin drop.

> To be back in Jamaica was special for Malcolm, even if his team was given no chance against a side that had ruled the world for the previous fifteen years.

'This is where I had grown up listening to the radio, to my hero Michael Holding or even the Australians Dennis Lillee and Jeff Thomson. I can still remember the commentator describing the run-up of Michael Holding as he hurled one down. I would go out the next day and do the same in the streets, on the beach or in the fields. Just try to bowl as fast as I could. My mum had died when I was six, and my father was in England because that's where

Malcolm's BEST BOWLERS

'Wasim Akram, Malcolm Marshall, Curtly Ambrose, Allan Donald, Waqar Younis and Glenn McGrath were all great, and you could learn something from each. But while you could learn something, it didn't mean you could bowl with the same effect. Any young fast bowler starts by trying to copy the style of their favourite quick, which was exactly what I tried to do.'

the work was, so I was raised by my grandparents. They encouraged me to live my dream, and all the way through I could bowl and run faster than most other boys.

'So that first wicket in the West Indies was a very big moment. I got 1/49 in the first innings and bowled okay, then in the second I got 4/77, including Viv again [bowled], Desmond Haynes, Gordon Greenidge and Jeffrey Dujon in a match we won. Nobody had given us much of a chance with all these experts predicting a 5/0 thrashing, but we had a good captain in Graham Gooch, who led by example. The West Indies ended up winning 2/1 but we could very easily have won the third Test in Trinidad.'

Had England won at Port of Spain it would have been largely on the shoulders of Malcolm, who produced 4/60 and 6/77 at a time in his career when he was encouraged to just go out and bowl as fast as he could. Later came the interfering types who attempted to correct an action that had pieces of Colin Croft in it, another of Malcolm's boyhood heroes who used to fall away sharply to his left in his delivery stride.

Devon Malcolm

> 'They encouraged me to live my dream, and all the way through I could bowl and run faster than most other boys.'

Malcolm's front was splayed as a result, but his shoulders were always strong and his pace the first thing batsmen noticed. One such batsman was Geoffrey Boycott, whose County side, Yorkshire, played a league side that included Malcolm. When Boycott had his castle destroyed he had seen enough to suggest to Derbyshire that they look more closely.

Towards the end of his tenure at Derbyshire, Malcolm was captained by Australia's Dean Jones. 'I captained "Big Dev" in 1996/97 at Derbyshire. He was one of the quickest of all time. People in England will always talk about his 9/57 in 1994 at The Oval against South Africa. This will sound strange, but he bowled unbelievably quickly when the sun was out. Often you see the real fast guys bowling at their quickest in overcast conditions. The other thing about Dev is he was still bowling serious heat when he was in his late thirties,' explains Jones.

'At his peak he was a very similar pace to Patrick Patterson, a young Waqar Younis, Wayne Daniel at times and Jeff Thomson in 1983 at The Junction oval when I was a kid. I know Thommo was well past his peak by that stage, but there was this one spell that still sticks in my mind. When these guys bowl at unbelievable heat it sounds like an arrow going through the air or the scratching of a match. Dev Malcolm got into the "oh my Lord" pace. He wasn't a bowler who wanted to hurt you before he got you out, but that didn't stop a few guys from taking backward steps from him.

'In the early stages of an English summer I think there were as many players who were scared to field in slips to Dev as there were to face him. Trying to catch an edge of his bowling could break your hand or

Devon Malcolm

Devon Malcolm on the receiving end from West Indian bowler Courtney Walsh. Sabina Park, Kingston, 1994.

fingers. I reckon with the really quick guys they all become known solely by their first names. There is Mikey [Michael Holding], Dennis [Lillee] Malcolm [Marshall], Curtly [Ambrose] and Dev.'

The 9/57 Jones refers to is the defining moment in Malcolm's career, the day the nice guy got angry and took it out on the South Africans. Malcolm had been ineffectual in South Africa's first innings, taking just 1/81 and refusing to intimidate tailenders Allan Donald and Fanie de Villiers with anything remotely short. His captain, Michael Atherton, was far from pleased at the break and let it be known.

So when Malcolm was struck on his helmet by a de Villers short ball, Atherton couldn't have scripted it better. The blow drew some chuckling from the slip cordon, prompting Malcolm to turn and deliver a warning along the lines of, 'You guys are fucking history!'

'When I came in to bat, one of the South African players said to Fanie, "Let him have one." I remember thinking they were just bluffing so I waited for the yorker, then he bowled this perfect bouncer that hit me. I was angry, no doubt, and while I might have bowled faster against the Australians on a couple of occasions, I did bowl quickly, and I bowled well. You never forget games like that.'

Devon Malcolm

HITTING BATSMEN

'I know this will upset Hoggy, but as a fast bowler you are trying to beat the batsmen with pace and you do worry when you hear that horrible crash on the helmet. You don't want to maim your fellow professional. You want to shake them, push them on the back foot, make them apprehensive. There have been a lot of broken bones over the years, I must admit: broken toes, fingers, arms; it's part of the profession.

When I was playing for Northamptonshire towards the end of my career I bowled to a young Middlesex player named Andrew Strauss. I bowled a bouncer to him, and he attempted to hook it. I walked down the pitch and said, "Young man, what are you doing?" He looked, but didn't say anything. I said, "We'll see." So the next ball I gave him a proper bouncer and hit him right between the eyes. If you look closely even now you will see a mark between his eyes where he had seven stitches. It's not what you want to do. I thought he showed real character, but he had to go off to hospital. I knew then he was going to have a long career. He was a nice guy and I felt ever so terrible.

Then there were some batsmen who cheesed me off, so it wouldn't have worried me as much. But I never seemed to hit them.'

Devon Malcolm

For the record, Malcolm took 9/57 off 16.3 overs, bowling South Africa out for 175. That set a total of 204 that England, with Graeme Hick on fire with a run-a-ball 81, reached for the loss of just two wickets, in the process ensuring the series ended 1/1. Malcolm shattered the stumps of two English batsmen and had five more caught behind the wicket by either keeper Steve Rhodes or first slip Graham Thorpe. His delivery to bowl Hansie Cronje was a peach, well through the gate before Cronje offered a textbook forward defensive stroke.

FASTEST BOWLING

'People will think of my 9/57 against South Africa at The Oval but there were probably a couple of times against the Australians where I bowled quicker. Against South Africa I had a bit of luck and every chance was taken, whereas against the Aussies at the WACA in 1995 I had match figures of 2/198, yet I definitely bowled faster. There might have been five or six catches dropped. In 1993 against Australia at The Oval I bowled very quickly. Dean Jones was my captain at Derbyshire and he reckons it was the only time he saw Michael Slater uncomfortable.

I was someone who required a lot of bowling under my belt and needed to play the games leading up to the Test matches. I just needed to feel the ball coming out nicely. Before that 1995 Perth Test I bowled really well on a flat Adelaide track to help win the Test. But I didn't always bowl well and I would be the first to put my hand up and say that. It was funny, but even when I was nearing forty I could still bowl really fast, maybe because I was fit and trained hard.'

Devon Malcolm

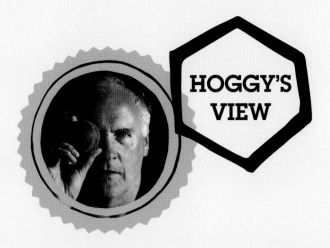

HOGGY'S VIEW

LOVED HIM, AND WHEN HE GOT IT RIGHT ENGLAND

normally won. He was a genuine strike bowler, not some medium-fast who bowled a heap of overs into the wind. I suspect he wasn't always used to full benefit, and he played in ordinary English teams so there weren't always a lot of runs to defend.

> On his day he surely rated with Harold Larwood and Frank Tyson as one of the fastest English bowlers.

At least Devon agrees with me that Viv was the most intimidating batsman to bowl to. And the thing with Devon is that he actually bowled while wearing glasses, just like Zaheer Abbas, Geoff Boycott and David Steele did when they batted. I'm impressed that Devon left that seven-stitch mark on the face of Andrew Strauss, but once again he doesn't appear to have wanted to hurt batsmen. I clearly must have been raised the wrong way. He is just such a nice man, and he was twice as fast as me even when bowling in runners. On his day he surely rated with Harold Larwood and Frank Tyson as one of the fastest English bowlers.

Devon Malcolm

SHAUN TAIT

'The Wild Thing'

Born 22 February 1983,
Bedford Park, Adelaide, South Australia

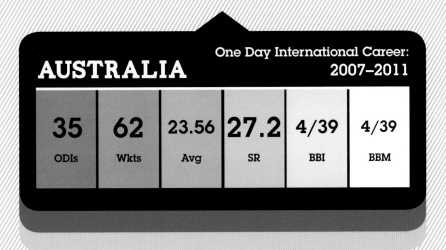

AUSTRALIA			One Day International Career: 2007–2011		
35	**62**	23.56	**27.2**	4/39	4/39
ODIs	Wkts	Avg	SR	BBI	BBM

Tait was a shooting star that flashed across the universe brightly and swiftly. But oh how brightly.

HAS THERE BEEN A BOWLING CAREER LESS GLORIFIED

by Test match achievement and yet so defined by sheer blistering pace as that of South Australian slinger Shaun Tait?

Others, the legendary West Indian pair Malcolm Marshall and Courtney Walsh, combined for 895 Test wickets, a mere 890 more than Tait, yet neither could say unequivocally that they regularly bowled with the same sustained speed. A man-mountain from the Adelaide Hills, nicknamed 'the Wild Thing' after the 1960s hit song, 195cm Tait captured the rock'n'roll of cricket 2000s-style better than any. He was a gun for hire who could produce speeds over 150km/h at will, but one whose fragile body reduced him to cameo roles around the world in the reduced format of Twenty20 cricket. If Frank 'the Typhoon' Tyson exploded and then left the international scene all too soon, Tait was a shooting star that flashed across the universe brightly and swiftly. But oh how brightly.

And just like another tearaway in Jeff Thomson, regarded by some as the daddy of them all when it came to sheer terror, Tait had a side-on slinging action, although it was not as fluent as Thomson's. But when he got it right, his high speeds were similar, something that began to emerge when he was nineteen. 'My action was natural, even though a couple of coaches tried to tinker with it. After a while they left me alone. Obviously it helped my pace, but it also put a lot of pressure on my body. When you can bowl fast naturally your captains want you to bowl as quickly as you can all the time. I have a big body, and my action put a lot of stress on it. When you try to bowl as fast as you can all the time then injuries just come with it.'

Tait grew up admiring the fast-bowling exploits of Craig McDermott, Waqar Younis and Wasim Akram. Like most kids he wanted to be an all-rounder, preferably in the Jacques Kallis mould, but his size always meant fast bowling could be a serious option. And the South Australian, who was built like an Australian Rules key position player, knew early on he possessed a weapon that may take him somewhere. 'I liked the fast bowlers, and because I was bigger I could do it. When I was about twelve, playing in the Under 16s, I filled in for a couple of games and didn't take any wickets but hit a kid in the nuts. I went away pretty pleased about it because he was four years older than me. I used to bowl outswingers when I was fifteen and was pretty accurate. Then I wanted to bowl faster, and my action sort of evolved. It was a matter of finding the best way to bowl fast, so I would try and copy a little bit of Brett Lee and Shoaib Akhtar,' says Tait.

Those who faced him in his peak years between 2005 and 2010 would suggest he not only copied those speed merchants to perfection, but at times outdid them. David Hussey, who has played all over the world at the highest levels for fifteen years, readily attests to Tait's potency.

'He probably takes three or four deliveries to get used to, but once you do, it's more the fear factor of getting through with the shot. He is the quickest I've faced. The night he bowled 160km/h against Pakistan at the MCG I well remember because I was fielding in the slips. I was behind the 30-yard circle, and that was the quickest I've

Tait's
BEST BATSMEN

BRIAN LARA

'I bowled to him a couple of times and I just couldn't work out a way to get him out. With his high backlift I thought I would get under his bat with a quicker one. But he would hurt you off the good balls you bowled. Lara and Sachin Tendulkar were the same: they would take you from off-stump and put you through mid-wicket or square leg for four. Even if you bowled at the stumps they would score off you.'

RICKY PONTING

'My big weapons were an inswinging yorker and bouncer. And he was so good at the pull shot that he took the bouncer out of my armory.'

BRAD HODGE

'A very confident bloke who was good everywhere. He would play dead-bat early on, and when the ball got old and wasn't moving he would do a lot of damage. When we had team meetings he was the only bloke in Australia we didn't really have an answer to. Even with the greats of the game you bowl straight early on and think you might get them LBW. But Hodge had every shot and he could adapt to all forms of the game.'

DAVID WARNER

'I struggled against Warner. I wondered how I could get him out if the ball wasn't swinging back in.'

Shaun Tait

Shaun Tait celebrates his first Test wicket after dismissing Marcus Trescothick of England. Trent Bridge, Nottingham, 2005.

ever seen. It was enjoyable fielding because you had so much time to see the ball. He was also moving the ball with very early away swing from the right-hander, although swing wasn't at the forefront of your mind – it was more the sheer pace and the fact he could hurt you.

'He is a real confidence player and if he gets a wicket in the first over, or doesn't get scored off much, then he goes from strength to strength. So in the shorter game we try to defend him in the first two, then hopefully use his pace to get a boundary. I would keep it simple, think fast, move fast, see the ball and bat on instinct. I wouldn't change my bat weight no matter who I was facing, from Shaun to spin. The next-quickest was Andrew Flintoff, because he bowled such a heavy ball that hit the bat really hard. I know Mitchell Johnson and Brett Lee are express-pace, but I didn't have the same issues because they had such pure actions and I got used to their actions quicker. Maybe I had that little bit longer to pick them up. I didn't face Allan Donald, thank god. I had trouble with Morné Morkel's height and steep bounce. With Dale Steyn I was more worried about the away swing than the pace.'

Shaun Tait

'I used to look at the speed gun a few times, particularly if the body felt good and I knew it was going to be a fast day.'

The game against Pakistan was a Twenty20 at the MCG in February 2008. By that stage Tait was viewed as more of a limited overs specialist, his at times fragile body unable to cope with the rigours of the longer forms of the game. He had taken a break a season earlier, unsure if he liked the rock star existence at the top of world cricket. On one hand there were fans and fame, on the other, his mates back in the Adelaide Hills who were just doing what young blokes do. But when he returned, his mind was clear and the carnage began.

'The "Wild Thing" nickname was a bit of a laugh. It came from Andrew Symonds, who really pushed hard for it after I started to spray them. I used to look at the speed gun a few times, particularly if the body felt good and I knew it was going to be a fast day. You couldn't help but look up at the scoreboard. You would give it a bit of a nudge to see how fast you could get, and I well remember a game at the MCG against Pakistan when I definitely looked up at the scoreboard,' Tait admits.

'It was a Twenty20 game when my speed was up in the high 150s, and I just thought for one ball I would give it everything. So I charged in and ended up falling over. But I got to 160km/h that day. I don't reckon the speed gun is always accurate. Sometimes you watch blokes and they seem slower, but come up 10km/h faster. The ball at Lord's when I bowled 161km/h, it felt like it was coming out well, so I knew then whatever I did it was going to be quick. That was a case of just bowling rather than deliberately trying to break speed barriers.'

The Lord's game was a One Day match in November 2008, when Tait went on a rampage at the home of cricket that will never be forgotten by those present, particularly English batsmen such as

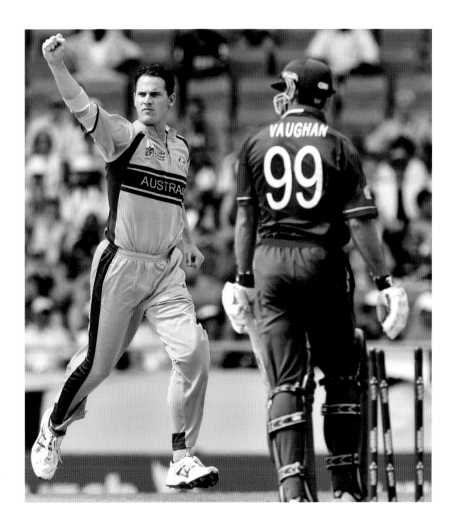

Andrew Strauss and Craig Kieswetter. He had one delivery timed at 161km/h, the first time anyone had been recorded at the magical mark in England. Former English paceman Angus Fraser had no doubt where Tait's sustained speed and 4/42 rated, claiming that 'Lord's has not seen as impressive [a] fast-bowling spell as this ever … and that's saying something when you consider how many great fast bowlers have performed here'.

Shaun Tait

He had one delivery timed at 161km/h, the first time anyone had been recorded at the magical mark in England.

After the game Tait explained he had 'left the handbrake off'. He admits he was particularly confident when bowling to the English, and had detected a couple were slightly nervous in their approach. 'Yeah, I thought I had the wood over Strauss and Kieswetter. I don't know if they were scared, I guess you would have to ask them, but the ball was swinging and I got the impression they didn't really want to be there.'

By that stage he was looked upon as an Australian player at both the One Day and Twenty20 formats. Arguably the zenith of his career was the 2007 World Cup in the West Indies when he was named as part of the fifteen-man squad, even if he wasn't a certain inclusion in the actual team until Brett Lee was ruled out with an injured ankle. Suddenly Tait assumed the role of key paceman, something he relished with 23 wickets at 20.30, including 4/39 off 10 overs in a semi-final against South Africa at St Lucia.

'That would have to be the absolute high point, looking back,' says Tait. 'I had a captain [Ricky Ponting] who backed me and told me I was going to be an important player in most of the games. It just gave me that extra confidence, and you have to remember I was playing in a really good side with some great players. It meant I was often bowling with plenty of runs on the board, and that took the pressure off. It was also a time when injury didn't worry me at all, which didn't happen all that often for me.'

He still rates the World Cup his finest international performance over a series. Still, playing Test cricket in 2005 fulfilled a childhood dream, even if he looks back now and questions whether he was ready. 'I would probably say I wasn't ready. I tore my shoulder that series, then had an operation and missed a lot of cricket after that. Had I stayed fit I might have gone okay after that series. I did okay in the first Test [3/97

Tait's
BEST BOWLERS

BRETT LEE

'I loved playing with Binga [Brett] Lee, so fast and confident. He was naturally fit and keep charging in and bowling around 150km/h. It isn't an easy thing to do to keep running in all day long. He did for all of his career. Binga bowled faster for a long period of time than just about anyone to play the game. Some might have been slightly faster, but did they last as long? And he was accurate. '

DALE STEYN

'Bowled fast and swung it away. And he is a nice guy as well, which will surprise some people because when he's bowling he's like a psychopath.'

MORNÉ MORKEL

'A really good bloke who just bowls fast and short. I love watching him. I got to know those players through the IPL. You learn so much.'

STEVE HARMISON AND ANDREW FLINTOFF

'In the 2005 Ashes series I shit myself facing Steve Harmison and Andrew Flintoff. Even our best players were worried by them. They had really good plans for us. Flintoff was intimidating. He got in our faces like we used to do. He had these massive hands, it made the ball look like a golf ball.'

and 0/24 at Trent Bridge] and no good in the second [1/61 and 1/28]. I wasn't sure if I belonged. It was just a pity I didn't get much chance after that. Apart from Clarkey [Michael Clarke] my teammates were all thirty or over. But they looked after me really well.

Shaun Tait

'Then three years later I got picked against India at the WACA. I did my hammy a couple of days before. The physio asked me if I was going to be right. I said, "I have been out of Test cricket for three years, so if I don't play now, I might never again." I didn't bowl well [0/59 and 0/33] and there was a lot of expectation. It was frustrating. I probably could have got myself fitter to have given myself a chance to play more Test cricket.'

HITTING BATSMEN

'When I started I used to like hitting people, and I would just turn back and walk back to my mark. These days when I have hit them I've gone up to see if they are okay. I have felt a little bit bad at times but as a fast bowler that's how you develop a reputation. If you hit guys, people start to talk about you. All coaches want bowlers who can hit guys. If the slips see you hit a bloke in the shoulder they get up for it. I don't think too many batsmen want to come in next, that's for sure.

When I was playing for Sturt in club cricket I knocked a bloke's teeth out, which was really nasty. He was a really good bloke but I guess you have to tell yourself it's all part of the game. On my first tour of Sri Lanka I was twenty-one years old and in my first proper net session. I bowled a short one to Ricky Ponting and he just didn't see it properly, and it hit him in the head. It gave him a cut, but he was fine. He was good to me and said, "No worries." I think he liked to see the speed I generated. I felt really embarrassed at first and thought, *oh no, what have I done?* But it was fine, and the boys were laughing at the end of it.'

Shaun Tait

194

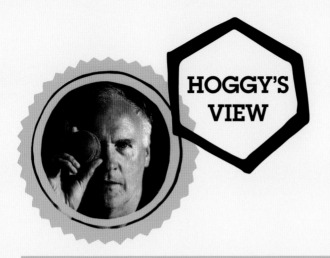

HOGGY'S VIEW

THERE ARE MOMENTS IN THE GAME THAT WILL ALWAYS

stick with you, such as Dennis Lillee's bowling in the 1977 Centenary Test at the MCG. Then there are those lesser-known moments, ones that aren't etched on an international level but unforgettable for those lucky enough to have been present. One such occasion was at the Adelaide Oval in 2007 when Shaun Tait was bowling against New Zealand in a One Day game. Adelaide is a ground where you get the perfect side-on view of the action because the square boundaries are so short. To see how far back the keeper was standing was such an exciting sight for an old fast bowler.

In terms of classical fast-bowling actions, Shaun Tait didn't have one, and no doubt it shortened his career. It was an action his body just couldn't maintain – with that action you could only be trying to bowl sheer pace because it's not as if a medium pacer would use it. His action would have been perfect if he was a javelin thrower in the Olympics where they have just six attempts. But we were asking him to bowl 15–20 overs in a day. And to his credit he kept running in and bowling as fast as he could. At his best he could also swing it, which at 155km/h is obviously hard to face. Of all the bowlers in this book he obviously has had the shortest Test career, yet he genuinely belongs because of his blinding speed.

Shaun Tait

JOHN SNOW

Born 13 October 1941,
Peopleton, Worcestershire

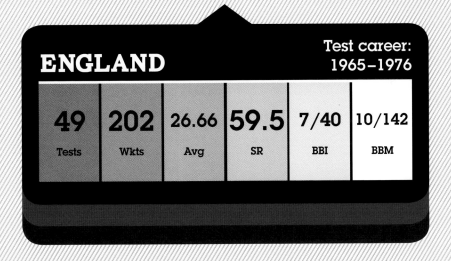

ENGLAND

Test career:
1965–1976

49	202	26.66	59.5	7/40	10/142
Tests	Wkts	Avg	SR	BBI	BBM

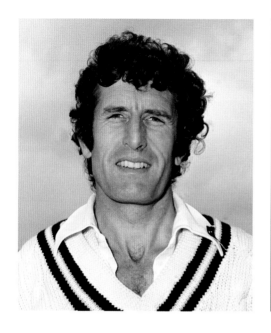

> 'If you really want to win, and I did, then you have to be bloody-minded.'

JOHN SNOW EPITOMISED THE GLADIATORIAL NATURE of the fast bowler. The vicar's son from Worcester with the slow-building run-up and radar-like short ball was easily able to leave friendships behind if they stood between him and a wicket.

And that extremely competitive nature hasn't faded with his seventy-three years. 'When people understood me, such as my captain Ray Illingworth on the 1970/71 tour of Australia, everybody worked in well together and there were no real problems,' says Snow. 'If you really want to win, and I did, then you have to be bloody minded. Ask my wife, she will tell you I'm bloody-minded,' he adds, laughing.

He remains one of the finest ever practitioners of the short ball. 'I used the bouncer to intimidate batsmen, and if they couldn't handle it then they shouldn't have been out there,' says Snow. 'I have never considered myself a mean person, but I could be hard if a batsman hit me out of the ground, as Clive Hubert Lloyd did one day at Trent Bridge.

'The Phillip Hughes incident was a freakish, tragic accident, something that all too sadly has happened twice in a hundred years. But as a

Snow's
BEST BOWLERS

FRANK TRUEMAN AND BRIAN STATHAM

'I used to watch Trueman and Statham and was a great admirer of them, particularly "George" [Statham].'

MALCOLM MARSHALL

'A great bowler, a man for all seasons.'

DENNIS LILLEE AND JEFF THOMSON

'Of course you can't not mention them. Dennis was a bit harum-scarum when he started out but you could always tell he had ability. During a rest day in the 1970/71 Adelaide Test, we all had a session down at a winery in the Barossa Valley where we talked fast bowling.'

GARTH MCKENZIE

'A fine bowler in terms of the mechanics of bowling fast and moving the ball. But when you bowl fast you need help, like anyone else on the ground.'

bowler you can't think about that because if you drop the bouncer then you are not really doing your job in testing the batsman. It's a psychological thing, the bouncer, and people will get hit and hurt – which is a part of the game.'

Snow, off a rhythmical run-up of eighteen paces that steadily built in its acceleration, wasn't the quickest bowler to hail from England. His pace is regarded as slightly inferior to that of Harold Larwood, and a good measure behind Frank Tyson – though most are when compared with 'Typhoon' Tyson. What Snow did possess was the ability to bowl at

John Snow

140km/h-plus for long periods, coupled with a short ball that seemed to have an instinct to soar towards the heads of opposition batsmen. He rarely bowled the wasteful delivery that passed harmlessly over the top, preferring the kind of chin music that was later made famous by the fast-bowling factory of the Caribbean Islands.

Australian stroke player Greg Chappell made his Test debut at the WACA in 1970/71, when Snow was at his peak. Chappell says the meeting changed his entire game plan.

'John Snow was a bit like Hoggy [Rodney Hogg], skiddy and never wasting any short balls. He was the first one who made me rethink how to play fast bowling. It was good that we got to bat against him early in our careers, before the West Indies came along. After he cleaned us up when they got the Ashes back in 1970/71, my brother Ian and I had quite a few sessions where we worked on hard wickets in the nets, throwing short balls so we could figure out a method to cope with them. There is no doubt it helped us deal better with the West Indies later on.

Unlike Hollywood heart-throb James Dean, Snow was a rebel *with* a cause, yet despite his obvious talent he wasn't always appreciated.

'To give you an idea of his pace, Snowy was in a similar category to Malcolm Marshall and Andy Roberts: sharp enough, and always asking questions of the batsmen. They were all thinking bowlers who had really strong shoulder actions where they generated their pace. It was hard to notice any difference in their action, and like Dennis Lillee they all had an excellent change of pace, being able to bowl that really quick one every so often. To give you a comparison, think Ryan Harris at his best – but with a better short ball.'

John Snow

As good as Harris has been in recent seasons for his country, he hasn't reached the heights of Snow on the Australian tour of 1970/71, when the curly haired part-time poet took 31 wickets at just 22.84 to help reclaim the Ashes, just as another pair of blistering pace men in Larwood and Tyson had done on tours before him. As with Larwood forty years earlier, Snow was the toast of English cricket before the same back-slappers in high places ensured his selection from then on was very much on their terms.

Unlike Hollywood heart-throb James Dean, Snow was a rebel *with* a cause, yet despite his obvious talent he wasn't always appreciated. Like his Australian rival, and later friend, Ian Chappell, Snow was firmly of

John Snow

the belief that the establishment was ripping off the cricketers. He determined in the early 1970s that whenever he noted buffoonery within administrative ranks he would make a stand. And given the nature of administrators at that time there were plenty of stands. Most cricketers today have little idea of how much rebellious figures like Chappell and Snow helped to pave the way for their lives as wealthy full-time cricketers.

Standing at 180cm tall with shoulders broadened by wood chopping and a three-year course studying physical education and geography at Culham College of Education, the young Snow was considered erratic with the ball. Like so many of his fast-bowling brethren, he did not earn a reputation as a tearaway in his early years, as the emphasis was on his batting – something that would help England and Sussex down the order in years to come, but not the skill for which he is best remembered. He was a handy rugby player at fullback and only an occasional bowler until a junior coach named Len Bates saw something in his action that others missed. Bates thought the fifteen-year-old kid 'bowled over the top' and had a natural run-up that built steadily in its intent. Yes, he could look lackadaisical with both bat and ball – and in the field for that matter – but there was something in that boy.

He started to scare batsmen out and his reputation spread, just as that of a hard-punching pugilist does in the local regions. At age seventeen Snow sent a visiting Dutch batsman back to his dressing-room after a short one reared and caught him on the head. It was a sign of things to come. In another game the opposition captain demanded Snow's removal before someone was seriously hurt. A few weeks later a batsman (unwisely, in hindsight, but with blissful ignorance at the time) reacted to a Snow bouncer by striding most of the way down the pitch to pat an imaginary spot just in front of the feet of the bemused bowler. One ball later the batsman was being carried off. Snow may not have aimed to hurt him, but a point had been made.

'You have to think for yourself, which a lot of players don't do. You can't just rush up and let it go. If you get hit for a couple of fours, you have to take stock a bit and get control back.'

These days, as a slightly mellower fellow who is widely respected and liked in the cricket world, Snow understands the mechanics of the short ball better than most. 'The bouncer is a matter of generating energy off the pitch, meaning you've got to get your weight and effort right to get it bouncing rapidly so that when you put it into the pitch hard it comes up steeply. You have to have a fairly high action for that and hopefully hit the seam to get more lift off the hardness of the seam. Even on a slow pitch, you always try someone out if they aren't sure about short-pitched bowling,' Snow explains.

'But there are other occasions when there is no point, such as with Hubert [Clive Lloyd] at Trent Bridge. You have to read the players, read the pitches. That is part of the art of bowling. So much of being a fast bowler is in the delivery of your weight. Your actual forward movement; your weight going over your front foot, which has to be abrupt; your muscle power; your arm speed and the use of your wrist just to flick the ball a bit. You have to think for yourself, which a lot of players don't do. You can't just rush up and let it go. If you get hit for a couple of fours you have to take stock a bit and get control back, bowl accurately and stop the guy from scoring so you are back in charge of what you are doing. Great fast bowlers keep on coming back, no matter what the score.'

And Snow was a great fast bowler, with the 1970/71 tour of Australia the pivotal moment in his career. One player who stood up to him was the ever-dependable and adaptable Ian Redpath, a skilled servant of Australian Test cricket who wasn't always treated with due respect.

John Snow

In that 1970/71 series, Redpath scored 497 runs in six Tests at 49.70, with Snow his main antagonist. In eleven Tests against Snow he fell eight times, yet there was mutual respect between the pair.

'He didn't move the ball a lot in the air, but off the seam,' recalls Redpath. 'He was very accurate and very awkward. Like Dennis Lillee he had that high action, and it all seemed to come easily for him because there was nothing expansive in his run-up. He also had that little bit of a temper that the great fast bowlers have, but like most he was a good fella off the field. I would place him in the top two that I faced, along with Wes Hall who was the quickest, clearly.

> These days, as a slightly mellower fellow who is widely respected and liked in the cricket world, Snow understands the mechanics of the short ball better than most.

'John Snow wasn't easy to hook, and I chose not to. But that was the same throughout my Test career, whether it be Mike Procter, who could be very lively, Peter Pollock, who was a fine bowler, or Andy Roberts and Michael Holding towards the end of my Test career. My old Victorian mate Keith Stackpole was someone who could hook Snow, and Ian Chappell, but Stacky [Stackpole] would hook a low-flying aircraft if the chance arose. Actually that isn't quite right because I did try to hook when I got to age forty and ended up getting hit in a district game by a good bowler named Andrew Scott of Prahran.'

Snow didn't hit Redpath on that tour, or any other time, but Graham McKenzie and Terry Jenner weren't so lucky, both being creamed by the Englishman who was at the peak of his powers. With left-arm orthodox spinner Derek Underwood typically keeping things tight

John Snow

from one end, Snow had the licence to attack. With Australia needing to win the final Test in Sydney to retain the Ashes courtesy of a drawn series, Snow cut loose. Australia's leg spinner Jenner, who was a handy batsman, misread a short one and ducked in to it, sending him reeling from the pitch. Umpire Lou Rowan issued a warning, and Snow responded by questioning Rowan's allegiances.

At over's end Snow made his way to fine leg to be greeted by cans and bottles from an undignified Australian crowd. One overly refreshed local reached across the fence and was captured in a now-famous photograph as he lunged and grabbed Snow's shirt. English captain Ray Illingworth, in an action that makes more sense as time goes by, took his players from the field and refused to go back out until the ground had been cleared. England returned and won the game to win the series 2/0.

Australia's Terry Jenner is struck on the head by a ball from John Snow. SCG, Sydney, 1971.

John Snow

Snow's
BEST BATSMEN

SIR VIV RICHARDS

'At Trent Bridge in 1976 Viv Richards got a few against us [232 off 313 balls] and he was a tremendous batsman.'

GRAEME POLLOCK

'Got to me at Trent Bridge in my second Test, which was a sobering moment.' [Pollock came in at 2/16 and left at 6/178 after scoring a majestic 125.]

ROHAN KANHAI

'Got a hundred [153] against us in 1968 at Port-of-Spain in Trinidad – simply a brilliant player.'

CLIVE LLOYD

'Ray Illingworth was my best captain for reading the game but when he suggested, or actually told me, to give Clive Lloyd one at Trent Bridge I explained, "I don't think it's quite the right wicket, Captain." And Clive then hit me over the stand.'

GREG CHAPPELL

'Got a century against us in his first Test in Perth and batted very well. Prior to that I had hit him at Hove when he was playing for Somerset, and I remember when he was picking himself up off the floor he said, "Don't ever tell me I can hook again." But I bowled bouncers at him after that and he flailed them.'

HOGGY'S VIEW

BEFORE THE CURRENT TRENDS OF REALLY TALL
bowlers in the 200cm range, John Snow had the perfect build. What was he, 180–181cm? Broad shouldered with strong upper thighs. I just loved watching him bowl with that economical run-up. He was so balanced and so tall at the point of delivery, and he could make a ball spit from almost a good length, which few bowlers have ever been able to do. He didn't waste bouncers, rather made them a thorough examination of a batsman's technique and intestinal fortitude. John Snow and Andy Roberts were the best bowlers of the short ball I have seen. Snowy wasn't a big swinger of the ball, relying more on seam and cut.

I actually played against him in Melbourne District cricket when he came over to play for Carlton in the 1971/72 and 1972/73 seasons, taking 72 wickets at 14.41. I was playing for Northcote in a two-day game over consecutive weekends and actually hit him on the shoulder. In those days they batted me at number six for some strange reason and I spent the entire week waiting to go in as we were three down at stumps. It rained and the game got washed out. Till that point in my life I had never been so happy to see rain.

John Snow

SHOAIB AKHTAR

'Rawalpindi Express'

**Born 13 August 1975,
Rawalpindi, Punjab**

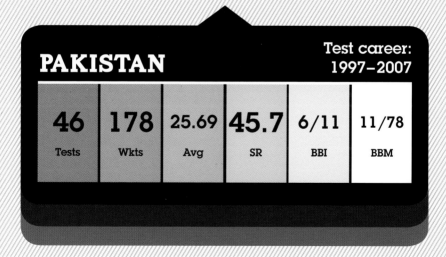

PAKISTAN				Test career: 1997–2007	
46	**178**	25.69	**45.7**	6/11	11/78
Tests	Wkts	Avg	SR	BBI	BBM

He brought
fear to opening
batsmen, though
he never caused
serious damage
to anyone.

SHOAIB AKHTAR'S LIFE HAS BEEN DEFINED BY SPEED,
from his childhood days in Rawalpindi to the moment in 2003 at
Newlands Stadium, Cape Town, when he delivered a 161.3km/h
thunderbolt against England in a World Cup match. Just as Ricky
Ponting is known for his pull shot, and Shane Warne for a ball of
deception called the flipper, Akhtar will forever be associated with a
sprinting run-up that wouldn't have been out of place in an Olympic
100m final and a delivery that could reach a blinding pace.

By breaking the magical barrier of 160km/h, which in the cricketing
world is the equivalent of a four-minute mile, Akhtar obtained his
nickname 'Rawalpindi Express'. He brought fear to opening batsmen,
though he never caused serious damage to anyone. He describes
himself as a 'kind fast bowler', one who was happy to frighten a
batsman into a false stroke, but who took no joy in hurting him.

That Akhtar became a 'son of speed' was due to a natural sporting
talent that saw him excel in hockey and soccer before cricket became
his game of choice around age fifteen. From the moment that

Shoaib Akhtar

Akhtar's
BEST BATSMEN

JUSTIN LANGER

'I found it hard to find a solution to get Justin Langer out. He was just so determined, so strong in the mind not to lose his wicket. We had some good battles and I respect him very much as a player.'

INZAMAM-UL-HAQ

'He was a player who never seemed rushed, one who had so much time. He did things in his own time; even in the nets you couldn't put him under pressure.'

RICKY PONTING

'When he was in form, most would be scared to bowl against Ponting. He never stepped back. I never enjoyed bowling to him because if I could not get him out in the first few overs, then he would make sure I would have to stay on the field for another 50 overs. He could take apart any attack.'

BRIAN LARA AND ADAM GILCHRIST

'Like Ponting they were both such damaging players that once they got in, you knew you could be in real trouble. So you had to get them early because they would change games.'

happened, his reputation quickly grew as stories of his awesome pace spread around Pakistan. His speed set the tone for his life, whether he was hurling human grenades at opposing batsmen or riding one of his fleet of high-powered motorbikes on the Islamabad Highway.

> Akhtar is said to have once driven a motorbike through the school principal's room.

Akhtar is said to have once driven a motorbike through the school principal's room while the master was present. He received three days' suspension, but it was worth it for the laughs and the fact he was the centre of attention – it seems this was the place young Shoaib often enjoyed being the most. But there were also quiet times spent on a rock near the family home, when he would imagine the heights to which he would climb in the cricket world. He must have resembled The Thinker, the 1880 sculpture by Auguste Rodin of a young man meditating while sitting on a rock.

Not that Akhtar was a thinker in the mould of Sir Richard Hadlee; as a cricketer, he was much more a young man who wanted to express himself through pace, and he bowled with that intent. Some batsmen handled him better than others, with Akhtar rating Australians Ricky Ponting and Justin Langer at the top of the heap, but none were entirely comfortable when the Pakistani was in full flight.

Akhtar was never more on song than in 2002–03, when he recorded speeds of 161.3km/h, 160km/h, 159km/h and 158.4km/h in spells against England, New Zealand and Sri Lanka. The 161.3km/h remains the fastest ever recorded delivery in an era where speed clocks are all the rage. And while Akhtar may not have been timed around 160km/h in a November 1999 Test match against Australia, nobody at the ground will ever forget an over he bowled to Ricky Ponting – least of all the Australian captain, who recalls the Rawalpindi Express running at full throttle.

'I had some great duels with Shoaib over the years,' Ponting says. 'To this day, I've always said he's the fastest bowler that I've ever faced in international cricket. There's one spell that everyone can watch on the internet of him bowling to me at the WACA. That was reasonably entertaining – more so for Justin Langer, who was at the other end laughing at me all the time when I was trying to keep Shoaib's deliveries out. He was express pace – a very, very good bowler.'

Ponting's long-time teammate Mark Waugh shares the view that there was nothing quicker than Akhtar when he got it right: 'On his day he was the fastest I ever faced. He was very difficult because of his pace through the air, and he could reverse it. When he was on song he was really good, but unfortunately for Shoaib it didn't happen that often, whether it was injury or the conditions didn't suit him. You got a good look at him during his run-up but I think because it was so long you only had to see him off for three of four overs.'

Brian Lara of the West Indies is hit by a bouncer from Shoaib Akhtar during the ICC Champions Trophy. Rosebowl, Southampton, 2004.

Shoaib Akhtar

Brad Hodge, a contemporary of Ponting and Waugh, and one who was restricted to just six Tests largely due to their presence, agrees with Waugh that Akhtar sometimes suffered from an inability to maintain his pace: 'Shoaib Akhtar was probably the quickest I faced, although I would say Shaun Tait could bowl faster for longer. With Shoaib you had to get past 10–12 balls so you could really get the pace. What scared you about him was the way he ran in from 40-odd meters back. You just knew it was going to be quick, and watching him run in played on your mind and allowed you to digest it. Akhtar was like Brett Lee in that you got a good look at the ball and seam.

'With those really quick guys it comes down to particular spells you face. Brett Lee bowled me two very quick spells whereas Shaun "Taity" Tait just about always bowled quick. And he could bowl 18–20 very fast overs in a day over three or four spells, whereas Akhtar had two or three. I remember playing for Australia A in Pakistan against Akhtar where his first spell wasn't that much, but then we lost a few wickets and in his second spell he really fired up and there was an instant change from 140km/h to 155km/h. And that is a dynamic difference, huge. Anywhere from 130–140km/h is manageable and comfortable if the ball doesn't move much, everyone is pretty equal. Anywhere from the 145–160km/h bracket eliminates everything and heightens the fear factor. You definitely lose some sleep the night before. I would change my technique, going right back into my crease to give myself a split second extra to see the ball.

'One of the real dangers with those really quick guys is getting bowled or LBW, so you learn to protect your stumps. The bouncer is dangerous but it generally doesn't get you out, so I concentrated on protecting the stumps and playing as straight as I possibly could with minimal backlift. But at that pace, they are all scary. The most dangerous bouncer I faced was Michael Kasprowicz, who wasn't the quickest but the ball just kept coming in at you with his arm angle, straight at your head.'

Akhtar's
BEST BOWLERS

BRETT LEE
'Brett Lee had smoother action than me; mine was a lot more difficult. Brett had an action that you would teach to children on the way up. And I respected him for being able to bowl fast for so long.'

SHANE BOND
'He had everything: beautiful bowling, pace, reverse swing, good action. I would also take the opportunity to watch him whenever he played on television. And then I met him and he is a lovely man. Injury stopped him from achieving greatness.'

Shoaib Akhtar

Hodge's Victorian teammate Shane Warne regards a particular spell from Wasim Akram as quick as anything he faced, but day in, day out, nominates Shoaib: 'He was the quickest. Ian Bishop was absolutely lightning before injury, and Patrick Patterson was very quick. Courtney Walsh and Curtly Ambrose were quick enough, and because of their height they seemed quicker – also because Ambrose bowled every ball at a perfect length and you couldn't get forward to him. His spell in Perth was the best I saw [7/25 from 18 overs].

'Shoaib and Taity had a similar type of slinging action where you couldn't really see the ball. Shoaib just hurled that arm behind so it was really hard to pick him up. Plus I was hopeless at the start of my innings, although extreme pace was probably better for me because I could cut and hook. I ended up standing with my bat up for the second half of my career. Graham Gooch did the same thing. Against Shoaib that gave you that little bit of extra time and, believe me, you needed it.'

> He could also swing the ball, although reverse was his main weapon.

Greg Blewett faced Shoaib in three Test matches in Australia in 1999 and averaged 51, yet never felt completely comfortable. This was particularly true in the first Test at the Gabba, despite he and Michael Slater putting on 269 for the first wicket. 'That was the quickest bowling I ever faced,' Blewett recalls. 'Shoaib was a fierce competitor but didn't say a lot and didn't need to when you are bowling at that pace, plus you just knew he was always after you. In a situation like that, you almost forget about technique and it becomes pure instinct where you try and react as quickly as you can. I obviously don't know if he was the quickest ever, but I do know it would be hard to imagine anyone quicker than his first three or four overs. He could also swing the ball, although reverse was his main weapon. And like Brett Lee and Allan Donald, he was a very good athlete.'

Shoaib Akhtar

216

English captain Michael Vaughan nominates a Shoaib Akhtar spell in Lahore in 2005 as the quickest he ever faced: 'I faced him bowling slower balls mixed with "superflex" arms so you lose sight of the ball. His double-jointed elbow made the ball disappear from his action and he was bowling like a javelin thrower. It was his intimidating run-up as well. He was reverse-swinging it and nipping it into the stumps. It's always easier if the ball is swinging away from the stumps because you have a chance of missing it, but if it's swinging into the body it is harder to play.'

New Zealand captain Stephen Fleming agrees that part of the difficulty in facing Shoaib involved the ball disappearing from sight shortly before he bowled: 'He was quite "slingy", and at times you could just lose the ball a fraction, sometimes a high arm, sometimes lower. He, along with Brett Lee, bowled a spell where I was a bit twitchy. He was

Shoaib Akhtar

very strong through his core. Shane Bond was a click below Shoaib but he could get it to reverse very early on at around 150km/h. Shoaib could reverse it as well, and at his speed you get exposed because you can't train for it.'

HITTING BATSMEN

'I was a kind fast bowler because I never wanted to hit a batsman. I would only bowl bouncers to try and get their wicket, not hurt them. I personally have never enjoyed it when I see someone go down and bleed because of my delivery. I felt very sad for Sean Abbott, trying to imagine the trauma that he went through [after Phillip Hughes died]. If I hit someone I would always run to them and hold them, as I didn't want to be scarred for life. People around Abbott would have helped him understand it was no fault of his and helped make sure he came out of it quickly and moved on, just as the game of cricket had to move on. In 2004 when I hit Brian Lara in the Champions Trophy, it was nearly in the same place as Phillip Hughes. So I thank god that Lara wasn't seriously hurt. And I hit South Africa's Gary Kirsten in a 2003/2004 Test when he was left with a bad cut on his face. I was very relieved when I realised there was no serious damage. I feel very fortunate that I haven't badly hurt someone and thank god. As for bowling quickly, it doesn't matter to me whether somebody recognises the speed gun or not – for me, it's satisfying that I have bowled the fastest-ever delivery.'

Shoaib Akhtar

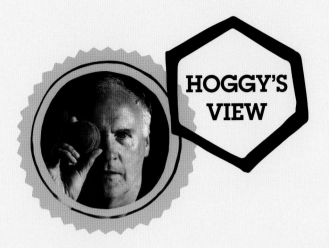

HOGGY'S VIEW

I CAN'T BELIEVE A BLOKE COULD RUN IN THAT FAST.
Shoaib looked like he was completing the Pakistani Olympic trials for
the 100m. The sight of him running in was one of the more stunning
things I have seen on a cricket field. You almost forgot he had a cricket
ball in his hand, although the batsmen having to face him didn't.
Had I ever faced Shoaib, I would have arrived at the crease in an
armoured vehicle, waved a white flag from the turret and retreated.
Batsmen might say he struggled to maintain his pace beyond three
to four overs, but nobody could run in that fast all day. You needed
to be in the prime seats for the start of play. He was an excitement
machine who gave us so much pleasure. Strangely he looked to me
more like a movie star than a fast bowler because he didn't seem to
have the build of a typical fast bowler. His sunglasses were never far
away, and he seemed to treat his hair with considerable respect, as a
superstar should. The game of Twenty20 was designed for Shoaib, for
his blistering fast overs. He was ahead of his time in that sense. I have
never seen anyone match his run-up speed, the closest being Dennis
Lillee in his early days and Michael Procter, though I think Shoaib
could run faster than Procter. And he could bowl faster than just about
anyone, although I still have this gut feeling that Frank Tyson and Jeff
Thomson might have been quicker in their day.

Shoaib Akhtar

RODNEY HOGG

'Hoggy'

Born 5 March 1951, Richmond,
Melbourne, Victoria

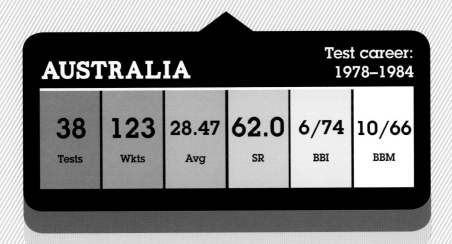

AUSTRALIA				Test career: 1978–1984	
38	**123**	**28.47**	**62.0**	**6/74**	**10/66**
Tests	Wkts	Avg	SR	BBI	BBM

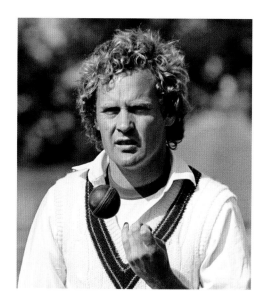

His future was decided after just five fast and furious overs from West Indian fast bowler Sir Wes Hall.

IT WAS AS IF THE SEAS HAD PARTED, SUCH WAS THE clarity of the moment for nine-year-old Rodney Malcolm Hogg on 18 November 1960. His future was decided after just five fast and furious overs from West Indian fast bowler Sir Wes Hall.

A young Hogg was awestruck at the sight of this magnificent athlete hurling bouncers and yorkers at Victorian openers Bill Lawry and Colin McDonald. Hogg had never seen anything like it, and while he was showing early promise with the bat, he determined he would one day rival Hall. He told his father on the way home to Thornbury, explaining that Superman and The Phantom were no longer his heroes. 'How can I look exactly the same as Wes Hall?' Hogg asked his father.

He was delicately told that while he could hopefully one day bowl as ferociously as Hall and possibly boast a similar physique, that god had made them differently in terms of colour. Temporarily pacified, Hogg still wasn't going to sit around and wait for his fast-bowling career to take off, so he began bowling at his father in their small backyard. 'I would run in as fast as I could and let Dad have it with a tennis ball. The short ball became my friend and I dreamt of striking batsmen. Then Phillip Hughes goes down and you think very differently,' explains Hogg.

Rodney Hogg

Hogg's
BEST BATSMEN

SIR VIV RICHARDS

'He was the best, and he actually intimidated me when it was supposed to be the other way around. I kept bowling short balls to him as I didn't have an outswinger and, as such, no plan B. And he kept hitting me for four or six. Then one day he missed and I hit him on the cheek – not a glancing blow. Viv didn't move, just stood there staring at me. So I walked to pick up the ball and see if there was damage to his handsome face. There was a cut on his cheek and I had visions of headlines: "HOGG DROPS VIV". But he didn't seem at all worried. Remember these were the days before helmets. Still he kept chewing and staring, so I picked up the ball and bowled another bouncer. It went eight rows back and after six overs I was taken off with 0/59.'

GREGORY STEPHEN CHAPPELL

'The second-best I saw.'

DAVID GOWER

'Batsmen who could score quickly … could demoralise me.'

BILL LAWRY AND SUNIL GAVASKAR

'They looked like their bats were illegally wide, such was their defence.'

ALLAN BORDER AND KIM HUGHES

'I loved Border's immense concentration, and Kim Hughes' courage and onus on entertaining.'

DAVID HOOKES

'The mystery to me is how he didn't succeed at Test level.'

Rodney Hogg

Hogg's
BEST BOWLERS

JEFF THOMSON AND ALAN HURST

'It was a waste of time and effort for Thommo to even bowl to me, I was so far out of my depth. On his day Alan Hurst was very quick, like anyone from the West Indies.'

RICHARD HADLEE AND DENNIS LILLEE

'Arguably Richard Hadlee was the best ever, although I would go for Dennis Lillee. Hadlee could make the ball talk.'

BOB WILLIS AND GARY LIVING

'Bob Willis used to scare me, and he knew it. He used to start laughing when I came out to bat. The bowler people won't know so well is Gary Living, who I played with at Northcote. I don't believe there has ever been a faster bowler at fifteen. He played senior cricket and in his first district game bowled Ian Redpath and John McWhirter, two blokes who hardly ever got bowled. Seeing the headline "Living and Hogg rout the opposition" was a real buzz. Gary played four games for Victoria then disappeared from the scene. He was going to be a star.'

JOEL GARNER

'He could be as fast as any of them – it depended on what sort of mood he woke up in. Had he been more disciplined at night time he could have been the best.'

KAPIL DEV AND IMRAN KHAN

'Watching Kapil Dev bowl fast outswingers made me jealous, and Imran Khan was poetry in motion. The difference between those bowlers and me was I would lose desire in places like England when the ball wouldn't get above the keeper's waist.'

Rodney Hogg

'But back then, before helmets, it was us against them. Trying to unsettle a batsman came naturally to me and I worked out early that most batsmen, other than Keith Stackpole and Viv Richards, didn't like accurate short balls. Maybe it came to me in the Under 13s when I was playing against the Fairfield Methodists and I hit one of their batsmen. After my over I went down to fine leg for a rest and suddenly this woman attacked me with an umbrella. It turned out her son was the batsman I had hit, so I could understand her being upset, even if I found her reaction extreme. I moved myself squarer out of her line of fire.'

The fuse had been lit and would fully emerge almost twenty years later when Hogg burst onto the international scene, playing for an Australian team weakened by World Series Cricket. Fast, straight and rarely wasting a short ball, Hogg set an Ashes record in Australia by taking 41 wickets at the remarkable average of 12.85.

Greg Chappell, who didn't play in that series but who captained Hogg after it ended, has no doubts about his capabilities: 'On his day Hoggy was as good as any of them. He just didn't have as many of the good days as he should have. Lenny Pascoe was a bit the same, a bit like Wayne Daniel in that when it clicked it came out very fast. Hoggy had

that skidding bouncer which was hard to hook, a bit like John Snow.'

Comments like that warm Hogg's heart, for deep down, despite the bravado he displays in his current role as a highly entertaining media performer, he is remarkably insecure about his place among the guns of Test cricket.

Former Australian opener Graeme Wood agrees that Hogg had it in him

> '**He needed to be controlled but he could be right up there on his day.**'

to be as quick as just about anyone, although he seemed to require extra motivation – unlike a Malcolm Marshall who just kept on running in and bowling really quickly, anywhere, anytime. 'If Hoggy didn't like the batsman at the other end he was really quick,' says Wood. 'In the 1981 series in England he didn't bowl one ball in anger until Ian Greig called him a cheat in a tour game against Sussex. When Greig came in to bat, Hoggy bowled as fast as I've ever seen anyone bowl. The problem was there were only two weeks left in the tour. He hit Greig then stood over him and said, "Cheats don't prosper,"' recalls Wood.

'In today's era he would have been sorted out a bit quicker, and would have played more Test cricket and been a much better bowler, but he was allowed to get away with too much early on. I played with him when he got his 80 wickets at 4.85 or whatever he goes on with all the time. In that series he was really sharp, but after three or four overs in one game he had 2/0 and wanted to come off. He needed to be controlled but he could be right up there on his day.

'Day in, day out, I think the quickest was Malcolm Marshall. He just bowled fast every day, and I don't think he knew anything but that. But the fastest bowling I faced was in a Shield game at the WACA playing for WA against SA with Joel Garner at one end and Rodney Hogg at the other. Garner just bowled like the bloody wind that day, it was incredible. And facing Hoggy wasn't much respite. For the West Indies Joel didn't get the new ball, so it was a different situation when he opened the bowling. For a left-hander Garner was the hardest to face. Andy Roberts had great pace variation and Colin Croft was difficult because of his angle. Michael Holding you could generally see pretty well.'

Rodney Hogg

Rodney Hogg

England's Geoff Boycott faces a bouncer from Rodney Hogg. MCG, Melbourne, 1978.

Hogg and Wood have remained friends, just as the fast bowler has with Queensland wicketkeeper John Maclean, who made his Test alongside Hogg at the Gabba on 1 December 1978. The pair shared in nine dismissals (all caught by Maclean) in the first four Tests of the series before Maclean was replaced by Kevin Wright. Hogg believes some of his 41-wicket success in the series was due to a number of lively tracks.

'My 41 wickets were on pitches that had a bit in them. And I was just that confident, thinking I would get a wicket every ball. Someone like Geoff Boycott you knew wasn't going to hurt you, so you could bowl six or seven overs, and while you mightn't get a wicket, you would only go for 0/10. The ones who worried me were those that scored quickly, whereas Dennis Lillee didn't worry about giving away runs, always trying to get wickets,' says Hogg.

John Maclean, sixty-nine, believes his old mate sometimes sells himself short and has no doubt his Ashes bowling in the summer of 1978/79 was right up there in the all-time speed stakes. 'Mate, I didn't know much about Hoggy before that 1978/79 series. In fact I can't even remember facing him in Shield cricket, but he certainly made an impression right from the start of the first Test at the Gabba,' says Maclean. 'He surprised Geoff Boycott, who had taken a two-year sabbatical because of Dennis Lillee and Jeff Thomson. Poor old Boycott came back and copped Hoggy, which was hardly any easier.

'Plus Boycott benefited from a couple of horrendous umpiring decisions off Hoggy. There was one nick that you could have heard in Melbourne, it was that loud. We lost that series 5/1 yet could easily have won it on the back of Hoggy. We were 2/1 down before the fourth Test in Sydney, where we led by 150-odd after the first innings. Geoff Dymock had Derek Randall as plumb as you will ever see but he was given not out and made 150. Had he been given out, Hoggy would have gone through the rest. We lost by 93 runs. Randall was as mad as a cut snake. He would keep marking the crease to Hoggy and drive him mad.

> John Maclean believes his old mate sometimes sells himself short.

'Hoggy never spoke much, he just stared and gave them plenty with the ball. He has those mad staring eyes, just like Gorden Tallis. I was made his fitness director in Melbourne and we won the match with him taking 10 wickets, but he didn't do much training. He was quick, skiddy and extremely difficult to face. He bowled either fast and straight, or short and accurate. I think he actually got it to reverse in that series before anyone knew what reverse was. He mightn't have bowled a big outswinger – in fact, like Thommo, I'm not sure he knew which side to hold the ball – but at his pace you only needed to move it a couple of inches. He was not as quick as Jeff Thomson, but on his day not that far behind. I would put Hoggy just ahead of Alan Hurst, who could be very slippery. Hoggy would have been over 150km/h in that 1978/79 series. No doubt.'

Rodney Hogg

HITTING BATSMEN

'I think I ended up hitting about forty. There was a time when I took a perverse pleasure in the number of batsmen I hit, but that all ended the day Phillip Hughes went down. It made me embarrassed that I had thought that way. I can remember playing for Warrandyte in a Melbourne suburban game when I hit this young bloke and fractured his skull. He was in hospital for a while, and I should have gone to see him. Then there was an Indian man whose teeth I knocked out when we were playing Eastern Zone in India in 1979. He had come out to the wicket with this beautiful smile and kept saying how proud he was to be playing against Australia and in particular Mr Rodney Hogg. I let him have it and my first ball ploughed straight into his mouth. I actually cried after I did that, which shocked my teammates.

My most relevant strike was against the touring Englishmen on the 1978/79 game against South Australia. I didn't take that many wickets but I dropped Clive Radley and put him in hospital. It started my Test career and finished his. I next saw him in London in 2005, and his wife threatened to pour her glass of red wine over me. He wasn't all that warm to me either, so I got out of there. But to me the bouncer is a weapon and when you couldn't move the ball in the air or off the pitch, like me, then you needed everything you could find. I did know how to bowl an outswinger but to produce it I had to drop my pace back a little and pitch it up further, which often used to go through the covers for four. I said, "stuff the outswingers," and I stopped bowling them.'

Rodney Hogg

230

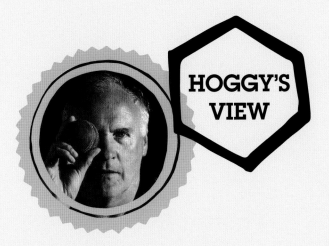

HOGGY'S VIEW

I'VE NEVER CONSIDERED MYSELF IN THE COMPANY OF THE others in this book. 'Typhoon' Tyson, 'Whispering Death' Holding, Sir Wes Hall, Jeff Thomson, Dennis Lillee: they're the great speed men. We weren't timed much during our careers so I don't know the pace I bowled, but I suppose on a given day I could get it up around 150km/h. I always wanted to be the fastest kid in town – I guess like the fastest gunslinger in the Wild West. But there was always someone quicker. In Grade Five, a kid called Michael Moet was faster than me. Then I went to Thornbury High, and there was a bloke called Frank Greenhaugh who was faster. When I went to Northcote, Gary Living was faster than everyone.

To describe myself, it would be as a one-hit wonder, someone who bowled quickly when it suited, meaning perfect conditions. The balls may have come out with a bit of pace in those circumstances, but conditions don't always suit and that is what separates the men from the boys. That's why we rave about Marshall and Lillee, because they did it in the extreme heat, on the fourth and fifth days. And I bowled too short – all my captains would keep telling me to pitch it up. Probably the only time I did in an entire series was the 1978/79 Ashes, and that's why I'm a one-hit wonder. A fair bit of seam in the wickets that summer helped every bowler. I also swore too much at batsmen, which comes back to being an only child.

Rodney Hogg

HOGGY'S TOP 10

Fastest Ever Bowlers
'ON A GIVEN DAY'

1. **Thommo**
2. **Tyson**
3. **Shoaib**
4. **Tait**
5. **Holding**
6. **Hall**
7. **Lee**
8. **Johnson**
9. **Lillee**
10. **Malcolm**

OUR FAST BOWLERS HIGHEST TEST WICKET TAKES

Test No.	Name	Wickets	Matches
1	Wasim Akram	414	104
2	Dennis Lillee	355	70
3	Allan Donald	330	72
4	Brett Lee	310	76
5	Mitchell Johnson	283	64
6	Michael Holding	249	60
7	John Snow	202	49
8	Jeff Thomson	200	51
9	Sir Wes Hall	192	48
10	Shoaib Akhtar	178	46
11	Devon Malcolm	128	40
12	Rodney Hogg	123	38
13	Shane Bond	87	18
14	Frank Tyson	76	17
15	Len Pascoe	64	14
16	Mike Procter	41	7
17	Shaun Tait	5	3

OUR FAST BOWLERS HIGHEST ODI WICKET TAKES

No.	Name	Wickets	Matches
1	Wasim Akram	502	356
2	Brett Lee	380	221
3	Allan Donald	272	164
4	Shoaib Akhtar	247	163
5	Mitchell Johnson	239	153
6	Shane Bond	147	82
7	Michael Holding	142	102
8	Dennis Lillee	103	63
9	Rodney Hogg	85	71
10	Shaun Tait	62	35
11	Jeff Thomson	55	50
12	Len Pascoe	53	29
13	Devon Malcolm	16	10
14	John Snow	14	9

Players without ODI stats played before the advent of ODIs. Statistics as of April 2015.

OUR FAST BOWLERS BEST TEST AVERAGE

No.	Name	Average	Matches
1	Mike Procter	15.02	7
2	Frank Tyson	18.56	17
3	Shane Bond	22.09	18
4	Allan Donald	22.25	72
5	Wasim Akram	23.62	104
6	Michael Holding	23.68	60
7	Dennis Lillee	23.92	70
8	Shoaib Akhtar	25.69	46
9	Len Pascoe	26.06	14
10	Sir Wes Hall	26.38	48
11	John Snow	26.66	49
12	Mitchell Johnson	27.84	64
13	Jeff Thomson	28	51
14	Rodney Hogg	28.47	38
15	Brett Lee	30.81	76
16	Devon Malcolm	37.09	40
17	Shaun Tait	60.4	3

OUR FAST BOWLERS BEST ODI AVERAGE

No.	Name	Average	Matches
1	John Snow	16.57	9
2	Len Pascoe	20.11	29
3	Dennis Lillee	20.82	63
4	Shane Bond	20.88	82
5	Michael Holding	21.36	102
6	Allan Donald	21.78	164
7	Brett Lee	23.36	221
8	Wasim Akram	23.52	356
9	Shaun Tait	23.56	35
10	Shoaib Akhtar	24.97	163
11	Devon Malcolm	25.25	10
12	Mitchell Johnson	25.26	153
13	Rodney Hogg	28.44	71
14	Jeff Thomson	35.3	50

Players without ODI stats played before the advent of ODIs. Statistics as of April 2015.

OUR FAST BOWLERS BEST TEST STRIKERATE

No.	Name	Strikerate	Matches
1	Mike Procter	36.9	7
2	Shane Bond	38.7	18
3	Frank Tyson	45.4	17
4	Shoaib Akhtar	45.7	46
5	Allan Donald	47	72
6	Michael Holding	50.9	60
7	Mitchell Johnson	50.9	64
8	Dennis Lillee	52	70
9	Jeff Thomson	52.6	51
10	Len Pascoe	53.1	14
11	Brett Lee	53.3	76
12	Sir Wes Hall	54.2	48
13	Wasim Akram	54.6	104
14	John Snow	59.5	49
15	Rodney Hogg	62	38
16	Devon Malcolm	66.2	40
17	Shaun Tait	82.8	3

OUR FAST BOWLERS BEST ODI STRIKERATE

No.	Name	Strikerate	Matches
1	Shaun Tait	27.2	35
2	Shane Bond	29.2	82
3	Brett Lee	29.4	221
4	Len Pascoe	29.5	29
5	Mitchell Johnson	31.3	153
6	Shoaib Akhtar	31.4	163
7	Allan Donald	31.4	164
8	Devon Malcolm	32.8	10
9	Dennis Lillee	34.8	63
10	Wasim Akram	36.2	356
11	John Snow	38.4	9
12	Michael Holding	38.5	102
13	Rodney Hogg	43.2	71
14	Jeff Thomson	49	50

Players without ODI stats played before the advent of ODIs. Statistics as of April 2015.

Acknowledgements

RODNEY HOGG

The concept of this book was formed in September 2014, prior to Phillip Hughes' tragic death. His passing is spoken of by a number of bowlers interviewed in these pages, who all agreed Hughes would be the first to say that the game must go on. Thanks so much to everyone for their contribution. I found everyone so humble. I am so proud to be connected to the fast bowlers union.

Rodney Hogg announced himself as the blond, blue-eyed, aggressive and menacingly fast bowler who took 41 wickets for the World Series-depleted Australia against England in 1978/79.

JON ANDERSON

Like Hoggy, I would like to thank all those great pacemen who were so giving of their time. In my case I was fortunate enough to spend a fascinating hour on the phone with Sir Wesley Hall, one of the true greats of the craft and an inspiration for so many from the West Indian Islands that came after him. Then there was Shane Bond, an extremely humble Kiwi who could have been anything but for injury. But with no bitterness, just a friendly nature that was typical of all these men who created havoc throughout world cricket.

Jon Anderson grew up country Victoria and, like many other budding cricketers, wanted to imitate whoever was the flavour of the time. In the 1960s it was either swashbuckling batsmen in Australia's Keith Stackpole or England's Bob Barber, while with the ball in his hand Jon unsuccessfully attempted to copy the loping run-up of John Snow. Then it all exploded in the mid-1970s when Dennis Lillee and Jeff Thomson decimated the English and West Indies, before Thommo did his shoulder against the Pakistanis. Jon has been lucky enough to meet and write about his sporting heroes in his roles as a sporting journalist with the Herald Sun in Melbourne and as a sports commentator on radio station 3AW. His favourite fast bowlers remain Thomson and Lillee, his most underrated being New Zealand's injury-plagued Shane Bond.

Image Credits

MITCHELL JOHNSON

8. Ryan Pierse/Getty Images Sport/Getty Images
10. Paul Kane/Getty Images Sport/Getty Images
12. Ryan Pierse/Getty Images Sport/Getty Images
14. Hamish Blair/Getty Images sports Classic/ Getty Images
18. Ryan Pierse/ Getty Images Sport/Getty Images
21. William West/AFP/Getty Images

MICHAEL HOLDING

22. Evening Standard/Getty Images Sport Classic
24. Bob Thomas/Bob Thomas Sports Photography/ Getty Images
27. Bob Thomas/ Bob Thomas Sports Photography/ Getty Images
31. Bob Thomas/ Bob Thomas Sports Photography/ Getty Images
33. Patrick Eagar/Patrick Eagar Collection/Getty Image

WASIM AKRAM

36. David Munden/Popperfoto/Getty Images
38. Bob Thomas/ Bob Thomas Sports Photography/ Getty Images
41. Rizwan Tabassum/AFP/Getty Images
44. Adrian Murrell/Allsport UK/Getty Images Sport Classic/Getty Images
49. Ben Radford/Allsport/Getty Images Sport Classic/ Getty Images

ALLAN DONALD

50. David Munden/Popperfoto/Getty Images
52. Ishara S.kodikara/Stringer/Getty Images
55. Adrian Murrell/Allsport UK/Getty Images
61. David Munden/Popperfoto/Getty Images
62. Ben Radford /Allsport/Getty Images

DENNIS LILLEE

64. Central Press/Getty Images Sport Classic/ Getty Images
66. Adrian Murrell/Getty Images Sport Classic/ Getty Images
71. Adrian Murrell/Getty Images Sport Classic/ Getty Images
73. Bob Thomas/ Bob Thomas Sports Photography/ Getty Images
76. Keystone/Getty Images Sport Classic/Getty Images
79. Central Press/Getty Images Sport Classic/ Getty Images

WES HALL

80. Central Press/Hulton Archive/Getty Images
82. David Munden/Popperfoto/Getty Images
87. Dennis Oulds, Roger Jackson & Leonard Burt/ Central Press/Hulton Archive/Getty Images
90. Harry Thompson/Evening Standard/Hulton Archive/ Getty Images

MIKE PROCTER

94. Bob Thomas/Bob Thomas Sports Photography/ Getty Images
96. David Munden/Popperfoto/Getty Images
101. Bob Thomas/Bob Thomas Sports Photography/ Getty Images
102. Photo by Evening Standard/Hulton Archive/ Getty Images

BRETT LEE

106. Doug Benc/Getty Images Sport/Getty Images
108. Jack Atley/Allsport/Getty Images Sport/ Getty Images
111. Greg Wood/AFP/Getty Images
113. Hamish Blair/Getty Images Sport/Getty Images
116. William West/AFP/Getty Images
119. Hamish Blair/Allsport/Getty Images Sport/ Getty Images

SHANE BOND

120. Hannah Peters/Getty Images Sport/Getty Images
122. Phil Walter/Getty Images Sport/Getty Images
125. Hamish Blair/Getty Images Sport/Getty Images
126. Shaun Botterill/Getty Images Sport/Getty Images
129. Alexander Joe/AFP/Getty Images)

JEFF THOMSON

132. Patrick Eagar/Patrick Eagar Collection/Getty Images
134. Bob Thomas/ Bob Thomas Sports Photography/ Getty Images
138. Bob Thomas/ Bob Thomas Sports Photography/ Getty Images
142. Keystone/Hulton Archive/Getty Images
145. Bob Thomas/ Bob Thomas Sports Photography/ Getty Images

FRANK TYSON

146. Allsport Hulton/Hulton Archive/Getty Images
148. Express/Express/Hulton Archive/Getty Images
152. Popperfoto/Getty Images
156. Patrick Eagar/Patrick Eagar Collection/ Getty Images

LEN PASCOE

158. Patrick Eagar/Patrick Eagar Collection/
Getty Images
160. Mark Leech/ Mark Leech Sports Photography/
Getty Images
162. Patrick Eagar/Patrick Eagar Collection/
Getty Images
165. Patrick Eagar/Patrick Eagar Collection/
Getty Images

DEVON MALCOLM

170. David Munden/Popperfoto/Getty Images
172. David Munden/Popperfoto/Getty Images
175. Patrick Eagar/Patrick Eagar Collection/
Getty Images
176. Patrick Eagar/Contributor/Getty Images
180. David Munden/Popperfoto/Getty Images

SHAUN TAIT

184. Bob Thomas/Popperfoto/Getty Images
186. Hamish Blair/Getty Images Sport/Getty Images
189. Hamish Blair/Getty Images Sport/Getty Images
191. Jewel Samad/AFP/Getty Images

JOHN SNOW

196. Bob Thomas/ Bob Thomas Sports Photography/
Getty Images
198. Bob Thomas/ Bob Thomas Sports Photography/
Getty Images
201. Bob Thomas/ Bob Thomas Sports Photography/
Getty Images
205. Hulton Archive/Getty Images Sport Classic/
Getty Images

SHOAIB AKHTAR

208. Julian Herbert /Allsport/Getty Images Sport/
Getty Images
210. AFP/AFP/Getty Images
213. Mike Hewitt/Getty Images Sport Classic/
Getty Images
214. Aamir Qureshi/AFP/Getty Images
217. Indranil Mukherjee/AFP/Getty Images

RODNEY HOGG

220. Patrick Eagar/Patrick Eagar Collection/
Getty Images
222. Bob Thomas/ Bob Thomas Sports Photography/
Getty Images
225. Bob Thomas/ Bob Thomas Sports Photography/
Getty Images
227. Ray Titus/News Ltd/Newspix
228. Patrick Eagar/Patrick Eagar Collection/
Getty Images